Contemplating the CROSS

Tricia McCary Rhodes

BETHANY HOUSE PUBLISHERS
MINNEAPOLIS, MINNESOTA 55438

Published by Bethany House Publishers
A Ministry of Bethany Fellowship International
11370 Hampshire Avenue South
Minneapolis, Minnesota 55438

Printed in the United States of America

ISBN 0-7394-0142-4

To my husband and my mom.
I am blessed daily with the selfless love of Jesus
that you never cease to pour out.

TRICIA McCARY RHODES is a freelance writer and worship coordinator for New Hope Church in San Diego, California. Her book flows from twenty-three years of full-time ministry and a longing to know Christ more deeply. Rhodes lives in California with her husband and has two children.

For more information on her speaking and writing ministries, you may contact Tricia at

New Hope Church
10330 Carmel Mountain Road
San Diego, CA 92129.
Phone: (619) 538–0888, ext. 111
E-mail: Tpraynow@aol.com

ACKNOWLEDGMENTS

There are no words to acknowledge the debt I owe to my gracious Redeemer who gave His life for me. I will never comprehend the depths of His grace, and I can only pray that somehow He will choose to use His work in my life at the foot of His Cross to draw others to Him.

Many people have supported me, encouraged me, and loved me through the painful process of writing of Jesus' final hours. I am grateful to God for all of you.

To the New Hope staff: Thanks for your sustaining, prayer-filled reassurance, and for freely releasing me to write when God calls.

To my editor, Steve Laube: Your input from the moment we talked of my own journey to the Cross has been the impetus for all of this—I am blessed with the way God uses you in my life.

To Kevin Johnson: You are a man of integrity and compassion. I thank God for a publisher like Bethany House, whom you represent.

To Sherry: Thanks for being a second mom to Jonathan when we needed you the most!

To my sons Champ and Jonathan: You've weathered fast food more often than anyone should—your sacrificial support, patience, and unconditional love is incredible to me!

Finally, to my brothers and sisters throughout the world who face vile persecution and death in Christ's name: You are the ones who truly embrace the way of the Cross day in and day out. May the rest of us never cease to plead your case before the throne of our omnipotent Father.

CONTENTS

CONTEMPLATING THE CROSS

In 1831 in a tiny Eastern European country called Lithuania, oppressed Christians gathered to worship on a hill in the north, planting small hand-made crosses in the ground where they knelt. The tradition grew and at the end of the nineteenth century there were 130 crosses on the small mountain.

Years later communist officials, determined to destroy all symbols of faith among the Lithuanian people, bulldozed the "Hill of the Crosses." Wooden crosses were burned, metal ones used for scrap, and those of stone covered over with dirt.

The Soviet army guarded the hill, planning to flood the area so people could no longer reach it. Four times they were forced to bring in tanks, for after each demolition the Lithuanian peasants secreted crosses to the hill and, mysteriously, more appeared than ever before. "Bulldozer Atheism," as the Lithuanians dubbed it, lasted almost twenty years.

When communism fell and Lithuania became an independent state, people flocked once again to the Hill of the Crosses. Today over fifty thousand crosses stand on the small mount. People from all over the world come to worship in the tiny chapel there. One religious leader describes the site as "our prayer and gratefulness to the Almighty."

The Hill of the Crosses in Lithuania symbolizes well the indestructible power of the Cross of Jesus Christ. For two thousand years governments

have sought to obliterate its memory and cultures have tortured and murdered its adherents, but the Cross stands eternally above all powers and principalities. In Christ's death lies the only real hope for mankind, and by embracing it people from every nation have come to know and deeply love this One who gave His own life for them.

An Eternal Summons

Today and every day, God the Father extends an invitation; to schoolteachers and bright-eyed children, preachers and bartenders, car mechanics and accountants, college students and garbage collectors, gamblers and homemakers. It is an eternal and unchanging summons to kneel in the shadow of the Cross where He sacrificed His only Son, and make it our soul's home.

God beckons us to gaze in awe at what we see on Calvary's mount. He challenges us to bathe in the wonder of such love until we lay ourselves down weary with unworthiness, yet cleansed and renewed in the healing stream of blood He shed there. He entreats us to be transformed by the terrible glory of the Cross.

My Journey

A few years ago, God touched my heart with a desire to understand what really took place in the final hours of Jesus' life. I began a journey of contemplation,[1] in which I took small portions of the Passion narratives from Scripture and allowed their reality to settle deep within. What I thought would take a few weeks and prepare me for the Easter season, took over a year and transformed my life.

I had been a Christian for thirty-five years. Not only did my upbringing provide a solid understanding of truths like propitiation, atonement, sanc-

tification, and justification, it produced within me a deep reverence for the death of Christ.

We commemorated it monthly through Communion—I ate the bread and drank the cup in solemn obedience from my earliest years. As a child my favorite hymn was "The Old Rugged Cross." As an adult I loved Good Friday and wrote numerous dramas to help others appreciate the Crucifixion.

But in the quietness of contemplative prayer, the Cross took root deep inside me in a way I am at a loss to explain. I saw the suffering of Christ and began to grasp the vileness of sin in my own life. The eyes of my battered, bloodied Redeemer wounded my heart with a painful sore that has never completely healed. My antiseptic rendition of faith disintegrated as Christ demanded a response to what I had seen. I felt as if I had come to the Cross for the very first time.

Join the Endless Chorus

I pray that through this book you will find your own way to the Cross of Christ. The journey may be tender and terrifying, soothing and unsettling. As you set your heart to reflect on Christ's passion, you will relive His pain, hearing His voice as He hung there.

You will struggle with Him, feel His wounds, embrace His broken heart, and enter the darkness of His abandonment by the Father. As you bring every part of your being to gaze at the face of Christ, you will see Him dying—not merely for the world—but for *you*.

Before He spoke the world into being, God was in Christ, reconciling man to himself through the Cross (Ephesians 2:16). When history as we know it comes to an end, the Lamb who was slain will open the book of eternal life. At this very moment the heavenly host will proclaim from the

throne room of the living God, "Worthy is the Lamb that was slain . . ." (Revelation 5:1–12).

In coming to the Cross you join this endless chorus. As you share in the sufferings of our Lord, you will find rich and often bittersweet fellowship with Him. Perhaps one day you will proclaim with the passion of Paul: *I know nothing except Jesus . . . and Him crucified.*

The Basis of the Story

The heart of this book lies in the narrative descriptions of Jesus' final hours. I have written them in the present tense to encourage you to identify with Christ personally as the story unfolds.

These narratives are based on the facts of Jesus' life as told by four of His followers—Matthew, Mark, Luke, and John. God divinely inspired each of these men to record various events from his unique vantage point, thus providing a rich blend of perspectives.

Piecing the four gospels into one story is a challenge. Some details are found in every account, some in only one. The order of events may vary from book to book; therefore none of the gospels in and of themselves provide a clear chronology. They must be woven together in a reasonable fashion.

In constructing the story, I follow for the most part A. T. Robertson's *Harmony of the Gospels*,[2] tracking Scripture as closely as possible. I fill in dialogue, add detail from historical accounts of that time period, and offer insights based on medical analyses of death by crucifixion.

Before You Begin

This book provides a simple format for your journey to the Cross. However, it is only a guide. God will fill in the pages as He speaks to you personally. There are three parts to each exercise:

Reflect

This ensures that you have stilled your soul and prepared your heart for quiet interaction with Christ. It is extremely important to take this time, especially in light of our busy lives.

Read

First you will read key passages about Christ's final hours from one or more of the Gospels. A short narrative follows to help you enter the experience of contemplation. Use your own imagination to embrace the sights, the sounds, the smells, the emotional weight of the moment. Take the time to pause often as you read, meditating on the scene before you.

Respond

As you finish reading, allow God's Spirit to imprint His heart on your own heart. I have provided questions, meditations, Scriptures, and challenges that will draw you deeper into contemplation. You will want to keep a blank journal nearby in order to record your responses. Pray, sing, worship, be silent, write; anything that helps you respond to Christ in a personal way.

My Prayer

Perhaps this book will provide you with a better understanding of Jesus' final hours. But beyond this, my fervent prayer is that as you reflect on these events you will be unable to resist the passionate love that drove Christ to Calvary on your behalf. May God touch your deepest soul and brand you with the fire of His devotion as you contemplate the Cross of Christ.

Notes

1. See my book *The Soul at Rest: A Journey Into Contemplative Prayer* (Minneapolis: Bethany House Publishers, 1996), a guide to the process of contemplative prayer.
2. A. T. Robertson, *Harmony of the Gospels* (HarperSanFrancisco, 1932).

CHAPTER ONE
AGONY IN THE GARDEN

In the days of His flesh, He offered up both prayers and
supplications with loud crying and tears to the One able to
save Him from death, and He was heard because of His piety.

Hebrews 5:7

I remember the first time I saw my father weep. The scene plays itself out in my mind even now, forty years later. I sat at my little table, giving my dolls tea and cookies while Dad put new linoleum on the kitchen floor. He worked and I played, a comfortable rhythm filling the room.

Then I heard it—a moan, a sob. Running to the kitchen, I was taken aback by what I saw. Dad stood looking right through me, holding a piece of linoleum, crying: "It doesn't fit . . . it doesn't fit."

I can't remember what happened next, but I will never forget the helter-skelter effect it had on my once ordered world. I couldn't know then, as I have since learned, all the pieces that contributed to my father's emotional breakdown—the financial pressures, the long hours at three different jobs, the endless changes and unanticipated costs of remodeling an old house—to name a few. All I knew was that my daddy, my protector, my strong giant of a father had fallen apart. I was afraid.

This is the kind of fear we face as we encounter the Garden of Gethsemane. We resist looking too intensely at the parts of a story that shake our sheltered belief system. What do we do with a God who breaks down like

17

us? How do we handle His weakness, His desperate pleading, His seeming lack of self-control?

Before we rejoice that Jesus chose the Father's will over His own pain, we must look hard at the blood oozing from his pores. Before we wrap His anguish in reasonable explanations, we must comprehend His complete sense of isolation and abandonment. Until we're willing to confront the terrible trauma of Gethsemane, the Cross will exist as a symbol of our religion, instead of the very heartbeat of our faith.

1. THE BEGINNING OF THE END

He who knows not the Christ of Calvary knows not God, and He who does not thus know, knows not anything that is worth knowing.

R. E. March

Reflect

Quiet your heart before God. Seek to release the worries, cares, distractions, and decisions of your day into the Holy Spirit's hands.

Read Psalm 25:4–5 aloud as a prayer and invitation to the Lord. Invite Jesus to open your spiritual eyes in a new way. Welcome Him as your companion and guide on this spiritual journey.

Think about the Cross for a few minutes. What images come to your mind? Does the thought of the Cross touch you deeply or has familiarity with it produced complacency?

What would you like God to do within you through this journey? Write this out as a prayer in your journal.

Read

John 17:1–18:1; Luke 22:39; and the following narrative.

And He came out and proceeded as was His custom to the Mount of Olives; and the disciples also followed Him.

Luke 22:39

As was His custom ... These are telling words about where Jesus will spend his[1] final hours of freedom. The Mount of Olives is a familiar place. He has been here often; only a week ago descending from it on a donkey, the crowds crying hosannas, laying palm branches at his feet.

On the nights following the triumphal entry, while his followers found rest in homes preparing for Passover, Jesus most likely slept here. He didn't have to travel far, just a few hundred feet up a stone path off the Jericho road.

What consumed his thoughts in those lonely hours? Was he exhausted from long days of teaching and healing in the temple below? Did he struggle to summon enough energy to walk down each morning, knowing the demands for his touch would be endless and overwhelming? Tonight on this mountain great anguish awaits the Messiah, but has he agonized over the coming crucifixion here before?

The full moon illuminates the way, regal cypress trees swaying in the breeze against the sable sky. Surely a quiet gloom accompanies them; Jesus talking, the men trying to keep pace, not wanting to miss a word. Once in a while he stops and faces them, expressing wistful thoughts and distant dreams.

He speaks of love, his love for the Father, his love for them, and their love for each other. Perhaps the intimacy is unsettling. It takes time to comprehend such words. But time is running out. They move on, following their beloved Rabbi.

He stops near a gate, gazing at the starry host above him. Then he lifts his hands to his Father and prays a long, poignant prayer for these faithful few, disregarding their questioning looks. After searching their faces once more, the Son of God turns toward the entrance to the Garden of Gethsemane.

It is a beautiful place, the night air in the foothills warm, the breeze from the brook Kidron blowing gently. The Garden's huge, twisted-trunk olive trees are laden with fruit. At harvest, the olives will be pressed until precious oil fills the vats. This "place of crushing" is a fitting finale for the One whose life breath will soon be pressed from him.

As was His custom ... The Mount is fraught with familiarity, even to Judas, the missing disciple, who within a few hours will confidently lead the army of betrayers to the Savior's side.

Jesus surveys the city, for which he has known such deep compassion, one last time. What does he see? Families relaxing, stomachs full and hearts warmed by Passover celebrations? Children being tucked in and candles snuffed out? Is the air peppered with the rumble of conversation or outbursts of innocent laughter among friends?

Amidst all this, does Jesus behold a lost and dying world, ignorant of their own need, unaware of the price he will soon pay to find a place in their hearts? As he gazes into the darkness below, what grips his soul?

It is the beginning of the end. As night takes hold, the blackest days of Christ's short stint with humanity close in. Within hours all of history will be catapulted toward that event for which there is no turning back. The beginning of the end.

Respond

The journey to the Cross is one of introspection. It is a time for deep mourning over the sins we have committed, which nailed Jesus there. In Scripture, ashes were a sign of repentance (see Job 42:6; Jeremiah 6:26; and

Matthew 11:21). Many people begin their journey to the Cross on Ash Wednesday (first day of the Lenten season) by having a cross of ashes put on their foreheads to symbolize their repentance of sin and desperate need for a Redeemer.

Today, reflect on your own need for a Redeemer. Consider your personal sin and disobedience. Embrace a sense of mourning before God as you begin this journey. Through eyes of grief, receive the love of Christ who died for you.

When God has spoken or moved you in some way, write a prayer of response in your prayer journal. It can be words of praise, confession, petition, worship, or even question—just open your heart to your Savior.

A Prayer

Lord, let me walk with you through these final moments. Let me hold your hurt, live in your loneliness, and experience what it cost you. For somehow, in embracing your pain, I may comprehend your love. Perhaps by grappling with your grief, I can conceive of your commitment to me. And in dying your despicable death, I might gain my own soul. I do not ask this lightly. I know I cannot come to the Cross without being changed. Let me walk with you, Jesus—make me ready for the journey.

2. MAN OF SORROWS

In the Cross God is revealed not as One reigning in calm disdain above all the squalors of earth, but as One who suffers more keenly than the keenest sufferer—"a man of sorrows, and acquainted with grief."

Oswald Chambers

Reflect

Begin with words of thanksgiving to God. Thank Him specifically for everything your salvation means—what it has given you, saved you from, etc.

Write a prayer of thanksgiving based on 1 Corinthians 1:18 in your prayer journal. Ask God to speak to your heart today. Affirm His presence during this time of meditation and prayer.

Read

Matthew 26:36–38 and the following narrative.

And He said to them, "My soul is deeply grieved to the point of death. . . ."

Mark 14:34

The hour is late. Stillness settles like an eerie cloud over Jerusalem. As he enters the gate in the wall around Gethsemane, Jesus motions to Peter, James, and John to come with him. The others sit down quietly to wait—for what they do not know—as the three follow into the recesses of the Garden.

Jesus moves slowly, perhaps stopping to lean against a gnarled tree trunk. White knuckles protrude from tightened fists and his head hangs in weariness. Peter, James, and John glance at each other, wondering what to do. Their teacher has never been like this before. They saw him cry when his friend Lazarus died, and only a week ago as he entered Jerusalem. He sobbed out loud over the neediness there. Yet that was a strong cry—laced with sadness perhaps, but not despair.

This is different. Overwhelming sorrow consumes the Christ. Through clenched lips, he utters: *My soul is deeply grieved to the point of death* . . . , a beleaguered bellow from the depths of his being.

What must it be like to grieve to the point of death? The language here speaks of both physical pain and mental anguish. Jesus knows not only agony of soul, but feels life itself slipping away as distress distills in his veins. Perhaps he could die even now—simply close his eyes, let his heart break, and be swept into eternity's glorious gates.

Instead, he laments aloud the condition of his soul. *My soul is deeply grieved to the point of death.* . . . Does he hope to be comforted? Wish things could be different? Is all this a surprise to the omniscient One? Didn't he know before he came that his heart would tear in two? Does the omnipotent Son of God have no power over the pain that threatens to undo him?

As sporadic sounds waft through the air from the valley below, a deathly quiet pervades the Garden of Gethsemane. Jesus grieves. Perhaps John reaches out, but hesitates at the look of torment in his teacher's eyes. Peter looks around, ready to do something, anything to end this distress. Jesus' body begins to shake. The man James once thought would be king is now pale, gaunt, and powerless.

Man of sorrows and acquainted with grief . . . strange words to describe a Deity. But he had given it all up—didn't consider equality with God something to cling to. Now what must the Messiah think? Does he long for a taste of the days when angels sang and all of creation cried out to his exalted Presence? Would he shed his royal robes so readily, in light of this smothering sadness?

Is the love that once sent him spinning into a woman's womb faltering, even a little? A resounding *no* echoes through the halls of eternity. The wretchedness written on the face of Christ will play itself out to the bitter end. Anything less would leave God's children hanging in the balance, bound in the slave market of sin's great camp. This he cannot allow. In some strange

way, God the Father is pleased to crush his only Son.

And so as travelers below settle down for another night's sleep, God's eternal plan marches forward. Earth's countless inhabitants are oblivious to the waves of emotion crashing into the cosmic Christ, threatening to drown him with their force. *My soul is deeply grieved to the point of death* . . . , he mourns, but life goes on.

Respond

Wait in the stillness of God's presence for several minutes. Have you ever lost someone or something dear to you? Lifelong plans and dreams? Friendship? Mother? Father? Child? Think back to that time, or try to imagine the kind of grief that can only be described as agony—both physical and mental.

Consider the words Jesus spoke: *My soul is grieved to the point of death*. Hear His voice speaking them. (To grieve means to feel deep sorrow, to mourn.) What might Jesus have been mourning in that moment? Ask God to give you a sense of the kind of sorrow Jesus was experiencing as He spoke those words. Wait and listen.

Read (or sing) the words to the old hymn below. Contemplate the face of Christ in the Garden as you do.

Hallelujah, What a Savior!
Philip P. Bliss

"Man of Sorrows!" what a name
For the Son of God, who came
Ruined sinners to reclaim!
Hallelujah, what a Savior!

Spend some time in worship. Speak words of adoration, thanksgiving, awe, and wonder. Sing, lift your hands, kneel in praise for One who would grieve as Jesus did and yet go on.

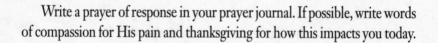

Write a prayer of response in your prayer journal. If possible, write words of compassion for His pain and thanksgiving for how this impacts you today.

A Prayer

Man of sorrows . . . You have looked sorrow in the face and wept in its wasteland. And though you grieved to the point of death, you did not die. Not then. O God, in the soil of your sadness, seeds of hope are planted for a dying world. Let me search deeply this moment of yours. Open wide my eyes that I might glimpse your eternal sacrifice. Take me into your dark night, and we will acquaint ourselves together with the paradox of grief's glory.

3. ONLY THE FATHER

The passion will inevitably remain extraneous to us until we go into it through the very narrow door of the "for our sake," because only He who acknowledges that the passion is his fault truly knows the passion. Everything else is a digression.

Raneiro Cantalamessa

Reflect

As you subdue your heart, gently thank God for being with you today. Take a couple of minutes to allow your soul to affirm Christ's presence here.

Read aloud Psalm 63:1–8, personalizing it as your own prayer. Ask the Holy Spirit to be your teacher and comforter through this time with Christ.

Meditate on the prophecies of Jesus found in Isaiah 53:1–3. Slowly speak each of the following phrases, contemplating what it may mean to you and a world condemned by sin.

- a tender shoot
- a root out of parched ground
- no stately form or majesty that we should look upon Him
- nor appearance that we should be attracted to Him
- despised
- forsaken of men
- a man of sorrows
- acquainted with grief
- one from whom men hide their face
- we did not esteem Him

What do you see in Christ that perhaps you haven't truly comprehended before?

Read

Mark 14:34–37 and the following meditation.

Remain here and keep watch with Me.

Matthew 26:38

Jesus moves away from these who have been his closest companions for the past three years. Yet he hesitates, perhaps wishing he could recapture the warm camaraderie they've known. He reminisces over Peter charging the ocean's waves in blind faith, and remembers the feeling of John's head against his chest as they dined a few hours ago. Recalling their naïveté and earthy take on life is like a soothing balm to the restlessness within his soul.

He searches their faces with a glimmer of hope. But there is little anyone can do now as spiritual forces in heavenly places draw their swords for battle.

The fate of his final hours flashes in front of him, and Jesus pleads: *Remain here and keep watch with me. . . .*

Such a simple request. Has he ever asked these men to do anything for him before? From the moment he called them from their businesses and boats, did he depend on them at all to meet his needs?

He fed the five thousand—first the disciples and then the multitude. Did anyone make sure *his* stomach was filled with the broken bread and dried fish? He calmed the wind when the night wore thin and their terror grew, but did any of them think to offer *him* a warm blanket or bowl of broth? A few hours ago he washed their feet—did anyone wash *his*?

He blessed the children, healed the sick, raised the dead, taught the eager, and loved the masses. Was there ever a time when he asked for help? A time when he felt his frailty and leaned on those who seemed stronger for the moment? A time like this one?

Moving a stone's throw away, Christ begins to wrestle with the Father's plan to redeem mankind. His cries grow louder and louder, but the men have fallen asleep. They hear nothing.

Remain here and keep watch with Me. . . . He asks for so little, but they can't give it. These ones to whom Jesus gave his every waking moment for three years cannot stay awake for one hour at his request.

After a while he rises. Unable to continue the vigil he crosses the few steps back to their side. John's eyes fly open, then drop in shame. Peter props himself up against a tree, determined not to let the Master down again. James wets his eyes with dew from the fallen leaves, longing to do the right thing. But when Jesus turns away, their heads drop as if drugged, escaping their own hidden turmoil. He stumbles back to the rock, his loneliness more intense than ever.

It must seem an eternity that Jesus agonizes in prayer before he returns, once again seeking his followers' nebulous aid. "Couldn't you even watch for an hour?" he asks.

What fills his voice? Frustration? Fear? Anger? Disappointment? Sorrow? No one tries to answer. There are no words left to speak.

In the end there is only the Father. He hovers near His child, though the agonizing dialogue between them is the start of a severing that will tear the Godhead apart. Visions of that moment torment the Son until he wonders if he can continue. He pleads with his friends, *Remain here and keep watch with me . . .* , but only the Father hears.

Respond

Sit quietly contemplating the darkness that surrounded the disciples that night. See Jesus a short distance from you, His heart beginning to break, His cries growing louder and louder. Imagine yourself falling asleep, oblivious to His pain. Hear Him gently calling you by name: *Could you not watch for one hour?*

Why do you think the disciples did not watch with Jesus? Why do you fail Him at times? Why were the disciples so out of touch with how terrible this time was for Christ? Are you at times out of touch with the true suffering of Christ? Why?

Ask God to give you spiritual insight into what Jesus was about to experience as He asked the disciples to watch with Him. Spend a few moments listening and examining on this.

Read Isaiah 53:1–3 aloud, slowly, one more time.

Write a prayer in your prayer journal using some of the phrases from Isaiah (e.g., *Lord, you were a tender shoot, like new life coming forth, fragile . . . and I crushed you.*)

Be quiet for at least five minutes, allowing this experience to settle within your heart.

A Prayer

O my Lord, I long to understand the extent of your isolation, the impact of your lonely pain. Did you ever feel at home during your stay on earth,

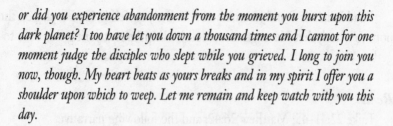

or did you experience abandonment from the moment you burst upon this dark planet? I too have let you down a thousand times and I cannot for one moment judge the disciples who slept while you grieved. I long to join you now, though. My heart beats as yours breaks and in my spirit I offer you a shoulder upon which to weep. Let me remain and keep watch with you this day.

4. IN STRUGGLE WE SEE HIM

Organized religion has domesticated the crucified Lord of glory, turned Him into a tame theological symbol. Theological symbols do not sweat blood in the night.

Brennan Manning

Reflect

Take some time to become still in God's presence. Slow your breathing through the following exercise[2]:

Inhale: Breathe in the peace of Christ.

Exhale: Breathe out anxiety of the day.

Inhale: Breathe in the gentleness of Christ.

Exhale: Breathe out mental clutter and distraction.

Inhale: Breathe in freedom in Christ.

Exhale: Breathe out that which binds you.

Inhale: Breathe in the joy of Christ.

Exhale: Breathe out discouragement.

Inhale: Breathe in the love of Christ.

Exhale: Breathe out selfishness and personal agendas.

Continue doing this until you feel ready to meet God according to His plan.

Read Isaiah 45:9 and Jeremiah 18:4. Offer yourself to God as clay on the potter's wheel, that He might accomplish His purposes during this time together.

Read

Luke 22:41–45; Matthew 26:42; and the following narrative.

And He went a little beyond them, and fell on His face and prayed, saying, "My Father, if it is possible, let this cup pass from Me; yet not as I will, but as You will."

Matthew 26:39

Jesus moves beyond his disciples, falling to the ground a few feet away. Pressing his face into the soil he once breathed into being, his body shakes in violent struggle. From the pit of his soul a child cries, "*Abba*—Daddy." He writhes, groans, and pleads for another way.

My Father, if it is possible, let this cup pass from me. . . . A heart-wrenching plea. Is this the Son of God? Weak? Frail? Fighting to hold on? Surely the Father longs to rescue him from this terrible plight. Can't the whole thing end right here? Perhaps, except for the words he summons the strength to add: "Nevertheless, not as I will, but as you will."

Throughout his life on earth, this is how it has been. Whether in the clamor and chaos of relentless crowds or the silence of solitary nights, Jesus has pursued the Father's will, for the Godhead celebrates a love affair unimaginable to human minds. Yes, for God so loved the world. . . . But the Son so loves his Father that he fights the darkness with a desire to obey.

The flesh-and-blood battle is real. It saps Jesus of strength, and twice he

walks away from it, perhaps to catch his breath or renew his determination. Each time he returns it is the same. Needy, frightened, childlike, he seeks another solution for sin-sick humanity.

The Father holds out His hand, but it clutches a bitter cup. Jesus glances into its depths. The contents would be vile, filthy, nauseating, even to those who have tasted sin. But to the Christ, whose heart is undefiled, the stench of it fills the air, the dark substance looming over him like an oozing sore.

His shaking intensifies. Perhaps he envisions himself taking the cup, drinking its bitter dregs until the poison of sin infects his whole body. His insides heave, catching in his throat.

A faint light to his side distracts him momentarily. Turning, he sees an angel. Is it Gabriel who announced his coming birth to a teenage girl just thirty-three years ago? The archangel Michael, sword drawn, ready for battle? Or is it an unknown seraph, sent to soothe his brow and comfort his suffering soul? Somehow Jesus finds strength in the presence of this celestial being and he prays once again: *My Father, if this cannot pass away unless I drink it, Thy will be done.*

With these words the full agony of it all sweeps through the Garden like a tornado, churning the body, soul, and spirit of the Son of God until he almost passes out. Bloody sweat from bursting capillaries pours from his face, large drops staining the ground.

All the forces of heaven and hell await the outcome of Christ's struggle in this place. Demons laugh at his weakness, angels weep at what he has become. The Father stands back, unwilling to intervene. Jesus faces poverty of soul . . . and eternity hangs in the balance.

Respond

Contemplate the faces of Jesus seen in this experience:

A child: scared, crying out in baby talk—*Daddy, Abba.*

A fully human man: feeling the terror of the future, pleading for another way.

An obedient Son: drawing from deep within to say, *Your will be done, Father.*

A fountainhead of love: looking into His Father's eyes and finding the energy to obey.

Try for a moment to imagine the cup the Father holds out. Look into it. What do you see? Observe your own sinful attitudes and actions swirling within. Think about the apathy and rebellion of the entire human race of every generation represented in that cup. See the kinds of sinfulness you encounter daily in your world—the violence, hatred, immorality, greed, etc.

Then consider the heart of Jesus as He looked deep within. What must He have felt? Why? What was the greatest source of His struggle?

What would your life hold today had Jesus dashed the cup to the ground, refusing to drink its bitter dregs? Don't rush with this question. Evaluate it deeply, pondering days and nights of an existence without redemption.

Write a prayer of thanksgiving in your journal. Thank Him that He loves you and that He loved the Father enough to obey.

Rest in the Presence of this love, allowing the truth of it to permeate your mind and soul.

A Prayer

Dearest Savior, I find myself wanting to run from your struggle. I'd rather see you fighting battles on my behalf, waging war against demonic armies. Maybe I'm afraid of what I'll see if I look too close at the cup you cried out against. O God, immerse my calloused heart in the dark waters of Gethsemane. Weaken me with the weight of my unworthiness, and perhaps I will glimpse my own soul in that vile and putrid cup. May I cry out in desperation as you did: "Abba . . . Father . . ."

Notes

1. I chose not to capitalize the pronouns referring to Jesus in the narratives, feeling it important to underscore the humanity of Christ in His final hours. In all other sections, references to Jesus are capitalized.
2. For guidance on this form of Christian meditation, see pp. 27–29 and the chart on pp. 37–38 in *The Soul at Rest: A Journey Into Contemplative Prayer*.

CHAPTER TWO

THE ARREST

*For He rescued us from the domain of darkness, and transferred us to
the kingdom of His beloved Son, in whom we have redemption,
the forgiveness of sins.*

Colossians 1:13–14

As a young boy in seventeenth-century Italy, Paolo Massari relished an unusual appreciation for the crucified Christ. His mother, having suffered great
losses in her life (including the deaths of ten children), taught him that the
strength to overcome all suffering and sorrow could only be found by embracing Jesus' death on the Cross.

Paolo came to Christ personally at the age of twenty-one and began to
pursue knowing Jesus with single-hearted devotion. One day in prayer he
had a vision that urged him to promote the memory of the crucified Christ
for the rest of his life.

For forty days he prayed and sought the face of God concerning this. As
he meditated on the Cross, he came to believe that the greatest work of
divine love ever known could be seen in the passion of Christ.

Following God's call on his life, Paolo ministered to the diseased and
dying and challenged the church hierarchy. For fishermen, woodsmen, shepherds, and spiritual leaders, Paolo preached one theme: the love of God seen
in Jesus' final hours on earth. He labeled himself a "Passionist," beginning

a worldwide movement of those who would devote their lives to identifying with Jesus' journey to Calvary.

No one really knows who first called Jesus' last moments His "passion." Perhaps it was taken from the Greek word *pascho*, which means *to suffer deeply*. This word was used often to describe Jesus' physical suffering (see Luke 17:25; 24:26; Acts 1:3; Hebrews 5:8, for examples).

It is a fitting description, for today "passion" means *unfailing devotion*. Jesus' walk to the Cross was the culmination of His life's unfailing devotion to pay any price for our sins. His passion demanded death—horrifying, gruesome, and intense.

Perhaps each of us who have tasted of Christ's saving grace can learn from Paolo Massari. Don't we all share his calling to promote the memory of Christ's death? When Jesus told His disciples at the Last Supper to *do this often in remembrance of me*, wasn't He instructing every follower to focus on the hours of His passion regularly?

Christ's unfailing devotion to redeem us began long before Calvary. We see passion in His arrest that night. We feel His concern for His young disciples and sense the strength of His determination to obey His Father. We embrace the anguish of a burning kiss by one He loved and experience the ache in His gut at being completely alone in time of greatest need.

Let us not rush even a moment of this troubling time we call the "passion" of our Lord, as we too embrace the greatest work of divine love ever known.

5. HUMAN ... AND WEAK

Only one act of pure love, unsullied by any taint of ulterior motive has ever been performed in the history of the world, namely the self-giving of God in Christ on the cross of undeserving sinners.

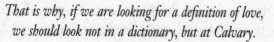

> *That is why, if we are looking for a definition of love,*
> *we should look not in a dictionary, but at Calvary.*

John R. Stott

Reflect

Spend a few minutes quieting your heart before God. Think of the word "passion." It means "unfailing commitment" and is synonymous with words like "ardor," "fire," "fervor." See Jesus with an ardent, fervent, fiery commitment to give himself up for you. Worship Him.

Read or review in your mind John 3:16. Meditate on the truth of this—try to imagine that this is the first time you have ever seen these words.

Write out a prayer of thanksgiving based on this verse, personalizing it (e.g., God, you loved this world—you loved me—so much that you . . .).

Read

Matthew 26:41; Mark 14:41; and the following narrative.

> *Keep watching and praying that you may not come into temptation;*
> *the spirit is willing, but the flesh is weak.*

Mark 14:38

The battle in the Garden continues to weaken Jesus, until it feels as if his very breath has been knocked completely from him. He gasps. Reckoning with the strength of his own flesh causes him to consider the three sleeping nearby.

Rising, Jesus studies their faces across the way. What does he see? Frailty? Naïve trust? Does he reflect on their inclination to falter when put

to the test, their weaknesses that he has come to know all too well? What concerns lie heavy on Jesus' heart as he watches them sleep?

There is James who, hours ago, sought to secure a status for himself that will never be. And Peter, who for all his bravado hides a little boy inside, often cowering in fear of failure. Sweet John, wanting nothing more than to love and be loved. All three sound asleep, oblivious to the horror the coming hours hold.

Does he feel compelled to warn them, to somehow get through to them before it is too late? *The spirit is willing, but the flesh is weak.* Only a few minutes remain—how can they possibly understand?

For two long nights they will face the darkness and try to deny that their Messiah has deserted them. The questions, the fears, the endless whys will tear at their budding belief systems. Hopelessness could creep into the empty moments and anger plant its bitter seeds. If his own battle to trust his Father is this fierce, how will they ever survive?

Jesus' voice echoes in the dark night with uncharacteristic harshness, like a parent fearing for his or her child's safety. *Keep watching and praying that you may not come into temptation; the spirit is willing, but the flesh is weak.*

How he must long to fortify their faith, to invigorate them with determination, to make certain they pray without ceasing through the hours to come. How hard it will be to leave them. The time together is almost gone.

Still they slumber, unaware of the intense emotion he experiences on their behalf. Turning away, he mutters almost to himself, "It's okay, go ahead and sleep . . . get your rest . . . you're going to need it."

What can he do after all he's done? What can he say after all that's been said? In a matter of moments they too will confront head on the grim reality that *the spirit is willing, but the flesh is weak.*

Respond

Meditate for a few moments on how Jesus felt, knowing what His disciples would be facing. Can you imagine the intensity of His concern? Con-

sider His compassion for them, even in the midst of His own intense personal struggle.

Read Galatians 5:16–17. Based on these verses, what battles do you think the disciples faced in the ensuing hours?

What struggles do you face even now to follow the Spirit? Is your own flesh weak? Contemplate the reality that Jesus sees every battle you face, especially when your faith falters and you cannot see God's hand. Look at your own life and spiritual journey. Hear Christ saying to you, *Watch and pray*. How will you answer?

Write a response commitment in your prayer journal.

A Prayer

Lord, in the midst of your own agony, your followers inhabit your heart. How you loved them. How you love me. And how you must grieve at my oblivion to the danger lurking in the shadows of faith. I, too, need your gentle admonition to watch and pray in a world that seems void of your touch at times. In the living of life—moment by moment, day by day—and when darkness tempts me to forget all you have said and done, let me hear your voice pleading gently: watch and pray.

6. RESOLUTION

Without Gethsemane, there would have been no Golgotha. The blood and water that flowed from His wounds on the cross were preceded by bloody sweat that poured from His pores as He suffered the agony of a death more painful than the physical death on the cross, the death of the will.

Michael Card

Reflect

Be still and know that God is present both within you through His Spirit and around you. Settle yourself for a few minutes with this thought. Welcome Him in your own words.

Read and/or sing the following old hymn as a prayer, preparing your heart to contemplate the Cross of Christ today.

O Love Divine, What Hast Thou Done!
Charles Wesley, 1742

O Love divine, what hast thou done!
The immortal God hath died for me!
The Father's coeternal Son
bore all my sins upon the tree.
The immortal God for me hath died:
My Lord, my Love, is crucified!

Is crucified for me and you,
to bring us rebels back to God.
Believe, believe the record true,
ye all are bought with Jesus' blood.
Pardon for all flows from His side:
My Lord, my Love, is crucified!

Behold Him, all ye that pass by,
the bleeding Prince of life and peace!
Come, sinners, see your Savior die,
and say, "Was ever grief like His?"
Come, feel with me His blood applied:
My Lord, my Love, is crucified!

Read

Mark 14:42 and the following narrative.

Arise, let us be going; behold, the one who betrays Me is at hand!

Matthew 26:46

Resolution. With forceful voice and rapid stride Jesus returns from his final time of prayer, startling the dreaming disciples. Demonstrating determination that eluded him a few minutes ago, he charges the impending doom, Gethsemane's agony behind him. *Arise, let us be going; behold the one who betrays Me is at hand!*

Exactly when did Jesus recover from his saga of blood, sweat, and tears? And did he spring to his feet with euphoric energy, or struggle to stand, stamina spreading slowly through his limbs?

The three look around in confusion. For the past week, hope and dismay have taken turns tossing them about as they watched and listened to their teacher. A few hours back he shared seder with them—a precious memory tainted by talk of a betrayer. But on the walk here to the Mount, he promised he'd be with them forever. Moments ago, through groggy sleep they'd heard him sob uncontrollably, yet now he strides toward them with confidence.

Arise, let us be going; behold the one who betrays Me is at hand! This is no weak resignation to fate. Does Jesus find strength in his compassion even for those gathering at the bottom of the hill, intent on his destruction? What propels him forward with such gritty tenacity?

Did something of cosmic significance occur as Christ cried the third time, "Thy will be done"? Did the heavens shake while angels sang songs of joy? Or did the moonlit sky echo back with Sovereign silence?

Nothing has really changed. The plan is the same. The stage is set, props put into place. The lead supporting actor executes the final details of his role as betrayer. And players move into position for the drama of all centuries.

Respond

What do you think went through Jesus' mind as He spoke the words, "Arise, let us be going; behold the one who betrays Me is at hand"? What emotions might He have been experiencing as He prepared for His own arrest? What kinds of thoughts do you think filled His mind? Spend a few minutes considering these things.

Three times Jesus described His final fate to uncomprehending disciples. He spoke of it with urgency: "And He began to teach them that the Son of Man *must* suffer many things" (Mark 8:31, emphasis added). Read Mark 8:31–35. Hear Christ's voice speaking these words to you as if you had never heard them.

What is He saying to you about your own life? What will it mean for you to accompany Him on the rest of this painful journey?

Respond in prayer to the challenge Jesus gives here. Write it out in your prayer journal.

A Prayer

Dearest Redeemer, even now you lead the way to your execution. Your strength sobers me, and I wonder how you prepared for this moment. I look at your determination to obey and weak excuses die on my lips. I want to walk with you still, though I wonder how close I can stay as you move to your death. If I turn away, gently remind me of this moment when you set your face like flint to the stormy seas that awaited you.

7. BETRAYED BY A KISS

And even so, with the meekest of gestures, has the war for the world been engaged. With a kiss. And the kiss has a tooth. And the snake that struck the Lord has a back of fire and a body of human opinion.

Walt Wangerin

Reflect

Read Psalm 32:1–2 slowly and thoughtfully. Read it again, placing your name in it. Reflect on what Jesus has done to forgive your transgressions and cover your own sins. Offer Him a heart of thanksgiving.

To betray someone is to be false or disloyal to that person. Ask God to reveal your own heart over the past few days. Have you been false? Disloyal to His call on your life? Ponder your own capacity to betray Christ day by day. Confess your neediness to Him and receive His forgiveness through arms held out to hold you.

Read

Matthew 26:47–49; John 18:2–9; and the following narrative.

But Jesus said to him, "Judas, are you betraying the Son of Man with a kiss?"

Luke 22:48

Jesus watches the steady snake of torchlights weave its way up the hill. As darkness holds back the dawn, a night owl hoots in the silent distance. Peter, James, and John shiver, shaking sleep from their heads. They summon the rest of the disciples, searching questions plaguing their minds. Where are they going? And why does their Master keep talking of betrayal?

So close yet worlds apart, a swelling crowd advances up the hill. The strange group shares an unlikely rapport. Roman soldiers, following orders to arrest some rabble-rouser, lead the way. Jewish high priests swallow their pride, knowing they cannot accomplish their goal without the help of "unclean" Gentiles. The temple guards follow, clubs and swords ready to meet expected resistance.

They all tread quietly—some full of haughty rage, some put off at having their sleep interrupted, still others following out of curiosity. In the middle of the crowd a Jew from the distant village of Kerrioth glances furtively about, nervous energy characterizing his movement. A couple of priests urge him forward.

Abruptly a figure emerges from the shadows. "Who are you looking for?"

The agitated Jew recoils, stepping behind a Roman soldier. The rest of the mob comes to a sudden stop, stumbling over themselves in surprise and fear. The military leader pulls himself together and barks, "Jesus of Nazareth!"

"I am he."

In tandem the entire crowd falls backward as if felled by a single stroke of lightning. After a moment's confusion, they struggle to their feet, baffled and embarrassed.

The quiet stranger asks again. "Who are you looking for?"

This time several speak up. "Jesus, Jesus of Nazareth."

"I am he. I am the one you look for—let these others go."

With these words, Jesus offers the betrayer a chance to walk away. The soldiers seem confused. They have come to arrest a hardened criminal, a dangerous interloper—not this unremarkable man who stands before them. No one knows quite what to do.

Except Judas. Jesus looks into the crowd, searching for his face. Slipping from the shadows, Judas throws his arms around his teacher.

"Rabbi." He kisses Jesus slowly—first on one cheek, then the other.

Judas, are you betraying the Son of Man with a kiss?

Time is suspended, the observers frozen in awkward stillness as they watch the painful interaction. Betrayed by a kiss. It could have been so much easier. Judas could have stood at a safe distance, pointing a finger while the

soldiers rushed in. He could have called out from afar, "That's the one—there he is, he's your man."

Does Jesus' face burn when those lips touch his cheeks? Does he kiss Judas back, holding him close for just a second amidst the crazy chaos of the night?

Judas, are you betraying the Son of Man with a kiss?

No reprimand. No rebuke. Just piercing words that rock the money keeper to his very core. The Redeemer reaches out in the face of lethal disloyalty and fixes forever his own terrible fate.

Respond

Try to imagine the scenes in the garden that night—disciples waking from restless sleep, Jesus intent on revealing himself, angry religious leaders and powerful soldiers forming a silent, but deadly mob, and one man embracing betrayal as a way of life. Place yourself there.

Sense what Jesus must have felt as the crowd approached. Consider what it is like to have someone you deeply love betray you by kissing you. Hear the tender voice of Jesus.

Read 1 Timothy 1:15. Meditate on this verse. See yourself as a sinner worse even than Judas in the moment he betrayed Christ. Feel the remorse over this. Offer a prayer of gratitude that Jesus receives you daily to His side, loving you unconditionally. Write a response in your prayer journal.

A Prayer

O my Lord, how many wounds you must receive on your journey to the Cross. This one must leave your heart raw. Betrayed by a kiss. I want to stand back and point my finger at Judas. And yet, how often have my lips burned your face with disloyalty? How many times have I reached for your touch, yet held my own heart at a distance? I long to say I will never betray

you Lord, but you know my heart. Hold me close when I do . . . especially when I do, for the road away from your side is a desperate one.

8. ALONE

My Jesus! Loaded with contempt, nail my heart to Your feet, that it may ever remain there, to love You and never leave You again.

Saint Alphonseus Liguori

Reflect

Take some time to set your heart toward God today. Acknowledge His presence and commitment to reveal himself to you.

In the Old Testament, a redeemer was one who, because they were re-lated to you by blood, could pay your debts and free you from the tyranny of wealthy landowners to whom you were enslaved. Jesus has redeemed you from Satan's tyranny and the darkness of his kingdom.

In light of this, offer Psalm 19:14 to the Lord, meditating on what it means to pray in such a way to your personal Redeemer. Write it in your own words in your prayer journal.

Read

Matthew 26:50–56; Luke 22:52–53; and the following narrative.

Then all the disciples left Him and fled.

Matthew 26:56

Jesus touches Judas' face, aching sadness pulling at the corners of his mouth. "Friend, do what you came to do."

Confused, Judas steps backs and suddenly everyone moves at once. Several grab Jesus as Judas slithers away. This carpenter has eluded them over and over again with answers they couldn't dispute and crowds clamoring for his touch. Tonight he won't find it so easy.

Time is of the essence, the cover of darkness their only hope for completing their plan. The blasphemer must be tried, convicted, and sentenced to death well before his foolish followers greet the morning light.

The disciples are stunned, paralyzed with shock. "What do you want us to do?" someone finally sputters, but Peter has already sprung into action. Tearing his sword from its sheath, he slices off the ear of one who holds Jesus' arm.

The high priest's servant screams, touching the warm liquid that drips down his neck. Tensions mount as fear fills the air. Something must be done to contain these crazy disciples at once. There cannot be a riot. Voices bark orders, but confusion reigns.

Then Jesus speaks, telling his men to put their swords away. Picking up the bloody ear, he restores it to the servant's head. He searches their eyes for a sign that they understand. How many times has he warned them of this moment? What will it take for them to realize that this is the way it must be? Don't they see the choice he is making for them, for the world?

They'd like it to be so simple, a clash of force. That kind of battle he could win in an instant. He glances upward, comprehending something they can't even imagine. Waving his hand across the misty air, he tries to explain.

"Thousands upon thousands of angels are ready this moment to wage war on my behalf. But I have a cup to drink. Can't you see that this is what the prophets foretold?"

The disciples hesitate, glancing at each other. Peter wipes his sticky sword on the grass, then puts it away. The others follow suit. A million ques-

tions tear at them, but there is no time for answers.

The priests, relieved at the respite, urge the soldiers to do their job. Several rush to Jesus' side, binding his hands with rough twine. He does not resist.

Then all the disciples left him and fled. One by one they disappear. Maybe they hide in the massive foliage of olive trees. Perhaps they hurry down a lesser-known path to reach the safety of their families. Even now they may mix with the crowd, unnoticed and unidentifiable as followers of Jesus of Nazareth.

He looks into the eyes of the religious leaders who have been dogging his steps all week. "Day after day I have been with you and you could have taken me then. This too the prophets said would happen—this is your hour and the power of darkness."

Offended at his arrogance, the priests press in, demanding swift action. The soldiers tighten the twine until it cuts into the flesh of his wrists, then shove him forward. Jesus glances around for the last time at the Garden he has come to love so well, looking for a final familiar face.

Then all the disciples left him and fled. Alone. Does he think of other solitary moments? His forty-day fast in the wilderness? Those quiet mornings in prayer down dusty paths of Jericho? Or long dark nights when sleep eluded him and he sought solace in the Father's arms?

Solitude is nothing new to Jesus, yet this is so very different. This time, He goes to lay down his life. This time he will not return to his disciples' side to teach and heal and touch their hearts with loving care. This is the end. And Jesus has never been more alone than in this moment when all the disciples left Him and fled.

Respond

Have you ever been alone, truly alone? Where there was no one to call, no place to go? Have you ever experienced extreme loneliness? Consider

what Jesus felt in that moment when they all fled. Think of all He had done and said to them. Think of all He will do in the coming hours. Muse on His pain.

Do you flee from the Cross at times? Do you tend to rush past the pain of the sacrifice Christ made, holding onto the power of resurrection?

It is the Cross of Christ that writes His love on our heart. Without a grasp of this, we will flounder and fail in our Christian walk. Read 1 John 4:10, 19. Have you really understood that we cannot love God on our own, can't conjure it up? We love because He loved us first. This is the message of the Cross. Write a prayer of confession, commitment, or worship in response to the Lord.

A Prayer

Dearest Shepherd of my soul, now you walk through the valley of the shadow of death . . . alone . . . so very alone. Did they scurry away from you like rats returning to the gutter of their existence? Did they even look back, or try to catch your eye one more time? You walk a lonely road, my Lord, and I feel the pain of abandonment in my own gut. I follow you . . . truly I do. Though none go with me, still I will follow . . . I pray it is so.

CHAPTER THREE

THE TRIALS

*But we do see Him who was made for a little while lower than the
angels, namely, Jesus, because of the suffering of death
crowned with glory and honor, so that by the grace of God
He might taste death for everyone.*

Hebrews 2:9

A painting by William Blake, artist and mystic, captures the essence of the Cross in a compelling way. It portrays a scene of utter darkness, except for a slim ray of sunlight illuminating Christ on the Cross. Below it stands a naked man with arms outstretched, an expression of deep longing on his face as he gazes upward.

This is the Cross—the only light in a darkened world, the only hope for desperate beings. Mankind, stripped of pretense and unable to hide from almighty God, reaches with yearning for a touch from the Redeemer who hangs there.

For two thousand years, volumes have been written about the Cross, scores of songs composed to tell of its glory, and thousands of artists have depicted its wonder through color on canvas. The Cross is not only the pivotal event in world history but must be the defining moment for those who believe in its power to save.

Yet we may study the Cross, analyze it, preach it, teach it, sing it, wear it, and display it in our home, and still maintain its symbolic status quo. How

can we get beyond superficial sympathy or even emotional fervor concerning the Cross? How can we transform our shallow grasp of Christ's death into a compulsion that drives us daily to the wounded One's side?

The answer lies in forging our personal path to the foot of the Cross. We do so by approaching Christ's final moments through the grid of our own life experiences. This can be a treacherous and tender journey, and one we must pursue with passion.

The trials leading up to the Cross are in themselves powerful reminders of God's sacrificial love. As you contemplate them, seek to rid yourself of nostalgic notions and comfortable conclusions concerning Christ's death.

See yourself afraid, following Jesus at a distance as Peter did. Consider how Christ could have cut His accusers to the core, but for you—He keeps silent. Join Herod in demanding signs of God's power, like an immature child wanting a show. Watch in sadness all that your Lord endures at the hands of evil men, knowing that if you were the only sinner, He would make the same choices.

Stand in the midst of the masses who cry out for His crucifixion, and determine to discover your place at His feet. Press on, push forward, pursue, and persevere until you are stopped short by the love in His eyes as He lays down His life on your behalf.

9. QUESTIONED

In all our lingering at Calvary, perhaps we are at no time more helpless
than when we attempt to survey the fullness of the Savior's love.
Calvary must speak for itself. Nor is it a mute testimony.
It is vibrant and vital in its expression. It speaks volumes.

S. Franklin Lodgson

Reflect

Engage in quiet reflection on your personal journey to the Cross thus far. What has God spoken to you in the quietness of your Spirit? Though it is a sad journey at times, what gifts of joy has focusing on Jesus' final days brought to you? Worship the living Lord who gave himself for you as you think on these things.

Read Ephesians 5:2. See the events of Jesus' final days as a fragrant aroma to God—an offering on your behalf. Write a prayer of thanksgiving in your journal.

Read

John 18:12–14; 19–23; and the following narrative.

He was oppressed and He was afflicted, yet He did not open His mouth;
like a lamb that is led to slaughter, and like a sheep that is silent before
its shearers, so He did not open His mouth.

Isaiah 53:7

The Roman centurion issues an official order to arrest Jesus of Nazareth as the soldiers slip a rope over his neck. Priests hiding their glee, hasten home to gather the high court. Jesus searches the faces that surround him. Does anyone look at him—really look at him? Do they notice the tenderness in his eyes or the lines of sorrow etched on his face?

Someone jerks the rope, plummeting Jesus forward. The fateful trip down Mount Olivet has begun. Only 100 feet below, mothers, fathers, sons, and daughters sleep off their Passover meal in peace, unaware of the catastrophic events to come.

The odd-looking group reaches Jerusalem quickly, taking care to keep their prisoner obscured from predawn worshipers. Down dark and empty streets the soldiers push and pull the Christ, void of concern for his welfare. *Like a lamb . . . led to the slaughter. . . .*

After a while they reach the palatial residence of the Roman governor. From daunting towers, guards observe the procession as it stops outside the gate. The soldiers, tired from the long night, await orders to return to their barracks.

For a while it seems as if everyone has forgotten Jesus. He gazes at the incredible architecture of Castle Antonia, knowing that it was built to protect the temple he will soon be accused of plotting to destroy. Does his heart grieve for the form of religion the temple now represents? For the rules and regulations that have replaced relationship with the living God in the hearts of his chosen people?

The clatter of conversation intensifies as leaders of the various factions argue over their next step. The priests insist that the soldiers' work is done, that this is a religious issue. Their own court is gathering even now to deal with it. Finally the soldiers give in, and once again Jesus is pulled along. *Like a lamb . . . led to the slaughter. . . .*

After a while the priests and temple guard reach two great palaces, side by side. They pause, unsure what to do. One palace belongs to Caiaphas, their leader, whose orders they now follow. But before that is the home of Annas, his father-in-law.

Everyone knows that Annas is the most powerful Jew in all Judea. Though no longer the official chief priest, he continues to rule behind the scenes with an iron hand. With five sons, a grandson, and a son-in-law as high priests, his influence is far-reaching. What would their chief priest emeritus think if he saw them leading the procession past his house?

At that moment, he appears on his bedroom balcony, beckoning them to bring the prisoner into his audience chambers. Eager to watch the old

master handle the situation, all of them scramble for a spot within the palace walls, thrusting Jesus to the front.

A hush fills the room as Annas enters. With beady eyes he scans the crowd, his gaze settling on Jesus. Glaring as if sizing up an opponent before a fight, his mind races. *Can this be the one? Can this be the revolutionary who has turned our city upside down—whose angry outburst in the temple cost me a day's profits?*

Annas considers for a moment what he might do to Jesus. How he'd love to handle this whole thing. But the law is clear. All trials must take place after dawn, with a certain number of Sanhedrin present. Finally he breaks the strained silence.

"Where then are your followers, Jesus of Nazareth? What has happened to those *men* you call disciples? Huh?" Annas sneers and shakes his head.

"And what exactly do you teach? Come, enlighten me."

Jesus ponders the question and for the first time since his arrest, opens his mouth to speak: "I've never tried to hide what I teach. You know I've been in the temple and synagogues—hundreds have heard me. Why don't you ask some of them what I have taught?"

A stinging crack fractures the uneasy tension in the room as one of the temple guards slaps Jesus: "Is that the way you answer the high priest?"

Annas, secretly enjoying the show, says nothing.

Jesus ignores the biting pain. This wound is one of many more to come, mild by comparison. He looks cautiously toward the guard. "If what I have said is wrong, then be a witness against me. But if not, then why hit me?"

Appalled at his audacity, the guard pulls back to strike again. This time Annas stops him, silencing the murmuring crowd. "Enough of this. Tighten his ropes and take him to Caiaphas. I have no more use for him."

And he who came to set prisoners free is bound once again. The Prince of Peace has become a spectacle, an evening's entertainment for the religious elite. *Like a lamb ... led to the slaughter ...* the carpenter from Nazareth

stumbles along, closing the curtain on one more scene in this desperate drama.

Respond

Consider the journey for Jesus—from Gethsemane to Jerusalem. Imagine being bound—pulled by a rope around the neck like a dog. Hear the jubilant cries of those who plotted His arrest. Feel the humiliation of being shoved in front of the chief priest. As you think on these things, remember that there was never a moment when Jesus was not choosing His own path— He came for this purpose.

Read Isaiah 12:1–6 aloud, thoughtfully, personalizing it. You may want to write a sentence of affirmation based on these verses in your prayer journal.

A Prayer

O Lord, they hit you—a stinging slap echoes in my ears even now. I want to cry at the injustice of it all. I feel your pounding heart, your swelling cheek. . . . Dearest friend of sinners, I too am one jerking the rope, pulling you closer to the Cross. My sins, my sins supply stinging slaps to your precious face. Keep me so close to your heart, that I may never get past this troubling reality.

10. AT A DISTANCE

You and I may give one another the impression of being earnest, godly Christians, but before the Cross we have to admit that we are not that sort of person at all. At Calvary the naked truth is staring down at us all the time from the Cross, challenging us to drop the pose and own the truth.

Roy Hession

Reflect

Prepare spiritually to hear God's voice today. Read Jeremiah 31:3. Hear those words spoken directly to your own heart by Jesus. In prayer, complete these thoughts:

Jesus, because your love is everlasting . . .

Jesus, because you have drawn me to yourself . . .

Jesus, because you draw me with acts of love and kindness . . .

Offer yourself to Him, as you return His love.

Read

John 18:15–18; 25–27; and the following narrative.

And Jesus said to him, "Truly I say to you, that you yourself, before a cock crows twice, shall three times deny me."

Mark 14:30

During the interrogation by Annas, the crowd in the courtyard has grown. A maid is assigned to watch the gate, opening it only for those with official business. Hearing a familiar voice, she turns and sees John, one of Jesus' disciples. Because their families have done business together for years, she lets him in, wondering why he would choose to be here.

Another man tries to follow, but she pushes him back. John turns and requests that his friend Peter be allowed to come with him. She shrugs, cracking the gate open. "So, you too, huh? Another follower of the carpenter?" she asks as he passes.

"Of course not." Peter answers and moves to a nearby fire, seeking to fit in with the rest of the crowd. John enters the palace to check on Jesus.

It isn't easy for either of them to be here. Putting their lives in danger, they have followed the crowd from a distance, down Mount Olivet and into the heart of the city, while others fled for safety. Peter's heart breaks at what they've done to his beloved teacher. He cannot leave now.

Yet he has just denied even knowing him. What does he think as he warms his hands? Why would this giant of a man fear the opinion of a court-yard maid? His heart pounding, he ponders his motives while trying to make small talk with the guards around the fire.

Suddenly one stares at him. "Why—you have the voice of a Galilean. You must be one of the prisoner's followers!"

Peter opens his mouth, uncertain what to say. Others join in. "Yes—you must be, or why would you be here at all? You're surely not one of us."

Peter bristles at the laughter that breaks out. "I don't know what any of you are talking about." He looks into their faces to see if they believe him, but by now they've gone on to another subject.

Trying to appear calm, Peter wanders to the shadows and sits down. Somewhere in the distance, a rooster crows. Again, Peter struggles. *Why have I done this? I've never been afraid before—I've fought my way out of more brawls than I care to remember . . . so why can't I tell the truth now and face the consequences?*

The minutes stretch into an hour. Peter looks at the eastern sky. No sign of dawn—will it ever break? And where is John? Why doesn't he come and give some word of their Master?

Inside the palace walls, John watches them tighten Jesus' ropes. He sees the bleeding lip and swollen face and knows it hasn't gone well. If only he could get his attention, just to let him know he and Peter have come. He tries to weave his way through the crowd, but the temple guards are pressing everyone back.

"Out—everyone out. We must go to the palace of our chief priest."

The guards move quickly, dragging Jesus in their midst. A bystander runs

outside to spread the news. "He's coming—they're bringing the prisoner through the courtyard to Caiaphas." Word spreads from servant to maid, from guard to priest, from fire to fire.

Peter's hands begin to shake. He has tried not to talk at all since someone recognized his Galilean accent. Suddenly the coals from the fire where he stands burst into flame, illuminating his face. He tries to back away.

"You—it is you! You're the one who cut off my uncle's ear when they tried to arrest the carpenter. You *are* one of his men."

Spewing foul and angry words, Peter denies ever having been in the presence of Jesus the Christ. But no one is listening now, a commotion across the way has caught their attention. The prisoner is being jerked and shoved through the courtyard.

Suddenly Jesus stops. For a brief second silence fills the air. He looks straight into the eyes of Simon Peter, his boisterous and bold, wild and wonderful disciple. What does he see? The wretchedness of shame? The hopelessness of failure? Does he long to hold Peter, to comfort him in some way, to reassure him of his love?

"Get moving," a guard yells, and the rope is pulled once again. Jesus moves on.

Peter feels as if his stomach has been turned inside out. He must get out of here. Pushing his way toward the gate, a distant screech pierces the raucous revelry of the crowd, stopping Peter in his tracks. A rooster crows for the second time.

Haunting words batter his mind, relentless words, sickening words: *You yourself, before a cock crows twice, shall three times deny me.*

Peter turns and runs, hot tears burning his cheeks . . . past the castle gate, down a dark road, running, running, running till he can run no more. Collapsing on the hard ground, he sheds bitter tears, remorse filling every fiber of his being.

He has failed his teacher, his Lord, his friend. And nothing can ever

soothe the ache in his gut, except perhaps a touch from Christ himself. But for now, that cannot be. Before this night is over, the Master will face the sentence of death. And Peter can only weep.

Respond

We often think of Peter as the one who betrayed Christ, but in reality, he was one of the only ones who stayed close to Christ after the arrest. What might have been his thoughts, feelings, fears as he followed at a distance? Place yourself in the courtyard that night. See yourself being asked about your relationship to Christ. How would it feel to deny Him, as Peter did? Do you at times deny Him by your life? Your words or lack of words?

Jesus was neither surprised nor discouraged at Peter's failure—He knew it would happen. In fact, after His resurrection, He sought Peter out. Their conversation is not recorded—just the fact that it took place (1 Corinthians 15:3–5). Imagine those moments together. If it were you, what would you want to say? To do?

Consider your own weakness, failure, and sin. Christ is not surprised or discouraged. Come to Him today to receive His love and forgiveness for all the ways you let Him down.

Write a prayer of response in your journal.

A Prayer

O Lord, how often I follow you at a distance. The cost of staying by your side is just too great. And I have denied you—maybe not with words, but in a thousand deeds of disobedience. I need to see your eyes of love across the courtyard of my life, but too often I find myself running away, burning tears coursing through my days. Seek me out, Lord—draw me to your side with the lovingkindness I sorely crave.

11. ACCUSED

You will understand that spitting scene that night
when God lets you see your own heart.

Alexander Whyte

Reflect

Prayerfully come before your Father today. Rest in His presence.

Consider for a moment that Jesus' death on the Cross was the ultimate sacrifice. Yet, in every event leading to the Cross, He continually lets go of things that are by all rights His. Read Philippians 2:5–8; 2 Corinthians 8:9. What specific things did Jesus give up in coming to redeem you?

Affirm these truths aloud, offering a heart of gratitude to Him.

Read

Mark 14:53; 55–65; Matthew 27:3–10; Luke 22:66–71; and the following narrative.

And the high priest stood up and said to Him, "Do You make no answer?
What is it that these men are testifying against You?"
But Jesus kept silent.

Matthew 26:62–63

By now almost the entire Sanhedrin gathers in the palace of their chief priest. Caiaphas is confident they will convict the carpenter from Nazareth of blasphemy. The law requires nothing short of death for such a charge. Feeling the blood coursing through his veins, Caiaphas flushes in anticipation.

Weariness is beginning to show on Jesus' face. He waits quietly while Caiaphas summons the witnesses. One by one they bring charges against him, but no two are alike. Every priest knows that the law requires two witnesses to convict.

Caiaphas scowls, calling for more testimony. Finally one man proclaims that he heard Jesus plotting to destroy the temple. Another agrees, but the details of their stories don't match.

Frustrated at the weakness of their case, Caiaphas addresses Jesus who has not yet spoken. "Do You not answer? What is it that these men are testifying against You?"

But Jesus kept silent. The entire council watches their leader to see what he will do. Things aren't going according to plan.

In a flash, Caiaphas sees his political power and social prestige vanish before his eyes. Filled with rage, he storms from his lofty chair, thrusting his bony finger in Jesus' face. "I adjure you, by the living God, that you tell us whether you are the Christ, the Son of God."

His voice echoes throughout the chamber. Jesus raises his eyes to Caiaphas. "I am. There will come a time when you will see the Son of man sitting at the right hand of power, and coming with the clouds of heaven."

"BLASPHEMY!" Caiaphas screams, as the room breaks into angry chatter.

He rips his cloak down the center seam, signaling his offense at Jesus' claims. How dare he quote the sacred Scriptures like that? How dare he speak with such audacity! He signs his own death sentence!

"We have all the witnesses we need right here! You have heard it for yourselves. What do you think?"

In unison they cry, "He deserves death!"

Chaos ensues. Some of the council crowd around Christ. Forming a circle, they begin to push him back and forth. Hands tied and unable to catch his balance, he stumbles, completely at their mercy.

Something wet hits his neck, then his chin, his cheek, his eye, until his face is covered. What must it feel like to realize people are spitting at you? To be the object of such utter contempt? To be incapable of even wiping off the filthy spittle?

One of the temple guards grabs his own belt and blindfolds Jesus. *Whack.*

"Who hit you? Tell us if you know—why don't you prophesy for us?" *Whack.*

Laughter fills the room. "Come on, *Messiah*. Tell us who hit you that time. Surely you know—after all, you *are* the Son of God."

Does he long to respond? Wish he could play their silly game, astounding them with his answers? Prove in this absurd arena his claim to deity?

Whack.

Whack.

Whack.

Jesus staggers with each blow, but those around him are enjoying their game too much to notice his weakened state. Dizzy and distraught by the pain, he gives in, letting them throw him about.

The wounds have begun in earnest for the sacrificial lamb. Vile and vain, the religious leaders taunt him . . . jeering . . . spitting . . . pummeling his face with their palms.

But Jesus kept silent. And like a sheep before his shearers, he opens not his mouth.

Finally they tire, drifting off in twos and threes to await the dawn. Caiaphas glances back at the battered prisoner. Let him be. He won't be going anywhere in his condition.

When morning finally comes, the guards rouse Jesus from his rugged sleep, dragging him to the temple for the "official" trial. This time they seek no witnesses as he stands before them. Caiaphas asks the salient question. "If you are the Christ, then tell us right now."

Carefully Jesus mouths an answer through lips split and swollen. "If I tell you, you won't believe me, and if I ask you, you won't answer."

At first the elders are put off. This won't do—it isn't blasphemy. But he goes on. "From now on the Son of Man will be seated at the right hand of the power of God."

Frustrated with the way Jesus' words seem to go in circles, Caiaphas cries out, "Well, are you the Son of God, then?"

"Yes, I am."

"Blasphemy! Let us take this impostor to our governor."

Among the worshipers in the temple courtyard, Judas shuffles anxiously about, regret eating at his insides. Upon hearing the verdict against Jesus, he bursts into the council chambers where a few priests remain, seeking to give back the money he earned for the betrayal, perhaps to assuage his guilt.

When they will have no part in his atonement, he throws the coins at their feet and runs out. As the priests contemplate this new development, a tormented Judas enters an empty field and hangs himself from a tree, branding the annals of history with his death. Guilt with no relief . . . sin without forgiveness . . . despair with no hope.

The death of Jesus too will stain the pages of perpetuity. Though he has no personal guilt to expunge or sin to atone for, soon he will hang from another kind of tree, spilling his precious blood for a world lost in darkness, and who knew him not.

Respond

Contemplating the details of Jesus' trial is a painful preamble to His gruesome death. But it is important to do so, because His suffering did not begin on Calvary. Spend a few minutes imagining the scene at the house of Caiaphas. Jesus chose to speak only at certain times, most of the time remaining silent. This greatly angered the chief priest.

Do you demand answers from Jesus that at times He chooses not to give?

How do you respond? With anger? Rejection? Discouragement? Lack of faith?

Contemplate what Jesus must have felt when the taunts began. Imagine the nauseous feeling of other men's saliva on your face when your hands are bound behind you. Think what it would be like to be one of those doing the spitting.

This is the living God, and there is no reason He should endure this kind of treatment. No reason except one—His love for you. Confess your unwillingness to accept Christ's silence at times. Pour out from your heart expressions of gratitude and adoration for your Savior who loves you with this kind of intensity. Write a few sentences of response in your prayer journal.

A Prayer

O precious Redeemer . . . what can I say to you—you who have been spit upon and ridiculed. You whose face is now misshapen by the blows of sinners. You who bleed, and fall . . . and yet utter not a word. I cry, but my tears seem a trivial testament to the torment you endure. What can I say? Nothing. Silent sorrow is my only recourse. I pray your heart can sense my grief.

12. THINGS HE COULD HAVE SAID

Christ is to us just what His cross is. All that Christ was in heaven or on earth was put into what He did there. . . . Christ, I repeat, is to us just what His cross is. You do not understand Christ till you understand His cross.

P. T. Forsyth

65

Reflect

In quietness, listen to the sounds around you. Seek to enter a sense of rest, letting outer noises become a distant hum. Set your heart toward the living God by expressing your thankfulness that He is always here, ready to meet you.

See 2 Samuel 7:22–23. Contemplate the greatness of God, especially in light of His commitment to redeem you. Pray, beginning with the words, "O Lord God, there is none like Thee who . . ."

Write it in your prayer journal.

Read

Luke 23:1–7; John 18:28–38; and the following narrative.

*And when he had said this, he went out again to the Jews,
and said to them, "I find no guilt in Him."*

John 18:38

By now the streets teem with morning worshipers. Many stop to stare at the odd procession. Jewish pilgrims recognize their most powerful leaders heading the parade. But who is the prisoner? Probably some poor beggar—clothes dirty, face looking like he barely survived a drunken brawl.

Once again Jesus is a spectacle. Some fall in line, forsaking worship to satiate their lust for the bizarre. There may even be an execution—why else would the Sanhedrin be bringing this one to Pilate?

What might Jesus see in the faces as he passes by? A mother whose tiny child he once brought to life? A teenager who sat one day on a hillside listening to him teach? An old man who shared in the miracle meal of fishes

and loaves? How do they respond when he catches their eye? Offer silent support? Turn away, embarrassed?

Outside Castle Antonia once again, the ragtag band stops. Refusing to enter the Gentiles residence and face defilement, Caiaphas sends for Pilate. Soon he appears at the top of the stairs near the gate.

"What are you accusing him of?"

The Jewish leaders irritated at Pilate's attitude retort: "If he hadn't done evil things, we wouldn't be here."

Pilate shakes his head. One more false messiah . . . one more fanatic claiming to be sent from God. When would these backward Jews ever stop their foolish games? "Take him then, and judge him yourselves."

Turning to leave, Pilate hears words he can't ignore. "He is guilty of death and we can't execute him. That is why we are here."

Sighing, Pilate gestures to his soldiers to bring the accused into the palace. By now he is curious—what could this plain man have done to stir them so? How powerful can he be?

"Well, is it true? Are you the King of the Jews?" Sarcasm drips from his voice.

"Did someone tell you this, or are you asking for yourself?" Jesus quietly responds.

"I'm not a Jew—your people, your own priests have brought you here. What in the world have you done to make them so afraid of you?"

"I do have a kingdom, but it isn't in this world. If it was, my followers would be fighting for power and control even now. If it was, I wouldn't even be here. But my kingdom is of another world."

Jesus' mystical rhetoric frustrates Pilate. He needs a simple answer to determine guilt. Why won't the man simply deny the charge, ending this whole fiasco? He tries again. "Are you a king then?"

Jesus looks off as if daydreaming. "I was born for one reason. I came into this world for one thing only—to speak the truth. Every person who rec-

ognizes truth hears what I am trying to say."

Bored, and eager to eat breakfast, Pilate rises.

"What is truth anyway?" he says almost to himself as they head back out to the palace steps.

Pilate looks down at the Jewish religious leaders who have given him so much trouble as Roman governor of Judea. "*I find no guilt in him.*"

Seeing their plan start to fall apart, the elders cry out.

"This man is trying to pervert our nation!"

"He refused to give honor to Caesar!"

Pilate glances over at Jesus, whose eyes are scanning the crowds that have gathered. "Why don't you defend yourself?"

"He says he is a king!"

Once again Pilate stares at the prisoner: "Don't you hear all they are saying? Why don't you answer these charges?"

There are so many things Jesus could say in this moment. *I am King of kings and Lord of lords! I am the Alpha and the Omega. For my own pleasure I created all things. I am the first and the last—in me every one of you lives and moves and has your being.*

But he says nothing, speaks not one word.

Pilate, marveling at the calm way the prisoner awaits his fate, proclaims again: "I find no guilt in this man."

Screams fill the air—loud, angry accusations.

"He stirs up the people everywhere he goes!"

"All through Judea he has been teaching and causing an uprising!"

Feeling loss of control, Pilate searches his mind for a solution to the craziness. He must have legitimate charges or Tiberius might hear of it and remove him from office. On the other hand, these Jews have caused so many problems with their fanaticism—what if they instigate a riot? How will he explain that?

"From Galilee to here, he has incited the people!"

"Galilee? Did you say he is from Galilee? Well, then, take him to Herod—he is here in Jerusalem too. Let him deal with the Galilean."

It seems a stroke of genius. First, Herod will be honored and perhaps put in a good word for him in Rome. Second, maybe he will take the Galilean home and try him there. Then all this will be a thing of the past.

Pilate turns to go, glancing briefly at the ill-placed prisoner.

Jesus, physically exhausted and weak from hunger, watches Pilate leave. The soldiers pull him roughly back down the stairs.

What does he hear in the midst of the crowd? Chatting, laughing, people excited at the turn of events? Lonely onlookers losing hope in the man they once thought would change their world? Religious zealots, meticulous about keeping the law, but lost at any rate?

Like a beating drum, the march moves on. Pious pilgrims prepare for their day of rest, and the plan for the Lord of the Sabbath turns another prophetic page.

Respond

Think for a moment about all the things Jesus could have said each time charges were brought against Him. Consider the things He could have done—to the Sanhedrin, Pilate, the soldiers, the onlookers. Given the reality that He was fully human *and* fully God at every moment, contemplate His ongoing choices to endure all that He went through.

Think of the people closest to you—family, friends. Hear Christ naming each one, saying, "For you I die." Hear Him calling your name, saying it to you.

Respond in loving words of worship and thanksgiving.

A Prayer

With accusations hurled about you, did you ever want to simply stop the whole thing—to whisper truth into the depravity of lies that filled the air,

my Lord? And I wonder where they were—those who might have defended you ... Nicodemus ... Josephus ... and your disciples. ... And where would I be if I were one of them? Give me grace to answer honestly, Lord.

13. HOPING FOR A SIGN

Come now my soul, and worship this man, this God. Come believer, and behold thy Savior. Come to the innermost circle of all sanctity, the circle that contains the cross of Christ, and here sit down.

Charles Haddon Spurgeon

Reflect

Breathe deeply as you affirm God's presence with you in this quiet time and place. Acknowledge your need for Him by confessing any sins that His Spirit brings to mind. Thank Him for healing and forgiveness that flows through His blood at Calvary.

Meditate quietly on 1 Peter 2:21–24. Write a prayer of thanksgiving for the specific things that Christ accomplished for you at Calvary.

Read

Luke 23:6–12 and the following narrative.

Now Herod was very glad when he saw Jesus; for he had wanted to see Him for a long time, because he had been hearing about Him and was hoping to see some sign performed by Him.

Luke 23:8

Sounds of dawn fill the air as Roman guards march the prisoner to the palace where Herod resides during Passover. The procession passes through the already bustling marketplace where people busy themselves setting up stalls. It is almost impossible to see Jesus now for the crowd that surrounds him—Roman soldiers, temple guards, high priests, and curious citizens with nothing better to do.

It is a short walk to the palace, but Jesus hasn't slept in at least twenty-four hours. Does he tire of the jostling, the tugging and pushing that prod him on when his feet falter? Does his head throb from the bruises of the night's beating? Or does he draw his reserve from some inner place of strength, a place no one has been able yet to destroy?

Troubling grief must occupy the heart of Christ as they approach the entrance. Here his cousin John was ordered beheaded because Herod's incestuous wife wanted him out of their way. Surely dread overcomes Jesus as he anticipates his encounter with the evil tetrarch.

At the palace, anticipation fills the air. Herod has wanted to see Jesus for a long time, having heard tales of miracles and bold teaching. Secretly, he fears John the Baptist has come back to life. Now he will be able to see for himself and do away with him for good, if necessary.

From the chamber where he waits, loud laughter resonates. Herod and his entourage can't wait to see this crazy man rumored to have raised the dead and turned water into wine.

When the somber group finally arrives, the prisoner is a disappointment. Disheveled, dirty, bruised, and bound, it is hard to believe he can perform miracles, much less entice whole villages to follow him.

Herod paces a circle around him.

"Who are you, really? And why have they brought you here?"

Nervous energy fills the air as Jesus fails to respond.

"Is it true you heal the sick? Raise the dead? Are you from God, or is all of this a hoax?" Herod stops directly in front of Jesus, demanding an answer.

There is none.

With growing frustration, he tosses out a variety of questions, none of which elicits a reply. Finally convinced that this couldn't be the brash John the Baptist, Herod tires of the fiasco. He looks around the room. As if on cue, the priests and scribes begin to call out angry charges against Jesus. Sputtering and fuming, they accuse him once again of blasphemy and treason.

Herod's soldiers, disappointed that they've seen no miracles, shake their heads in disgust and begin to ridicule him. "Mighty miracle man? You can't even untie your hands!"

"You can't do miracles—you're just a washed-up prophet."

A priest shouts above the mocking soldiers. "It doesn't matter what he is—he is stirring people up against the government. He is a threat to Caesar."

Herod laughs out loud. "Him—a threat? How could he be a threat to anyone? He's harmless . . . pitiful, a weak excuse for a man."

One of the soldiers makes a sweeping bow before Jesus, feigning submission. The others jeer as they kneel in mock subjection to the would-be king.

Herod joins in the gaiety, donning one of his royal robes and placing it on Jesus' shoulders. The sight of the bedraggled prisoner dressed as a king amuses even the high priests.

What thoughts must plague Jesus now? In this glorious palace does he reminisce over the magnificent throne he left behind when he came to a fallen earth? Does this beautiful robe remind him of the robes of white his death will secure for sinners such as these?

Which hurts most—the physical injuries from the beating the night before or the mental cruelty thrust upon him now? Knowing what he knows, how can he keep taking the abuse?

Suddenly bored with the whole thing, Herod turns to leave. "Take him back to *my friend, Pilate*. Tell him I find nothing worthy of death in this man."

An unusual alliance—Pilate, the Roman procurator and Herod, the Jewish tetrarch—who have been enemies up to this very moment. But politics make strange bedfellows, and another piece of the passion puzzle fits nicely into place.

Respond

Consider Jesus enduring this kind of ridicule. How did He do it? What sustained Him? In His humanity, what do you think He experienced in those moments?

See yourself as one of the soldiers, bowing in mockery before Him. Look into His eyes and seek to comprehend His thoughts and emotions.

Read 1 Peter 2:23 again. According to this verse, how did Jesus endure? Imagine His going through this process over and over again. Praise Him that He chose to go through it when He could have walked away. Offer Him your personal worship and gratitude.

A Prayer

King of kings and Lord of lords . . . they mock you. You didn't perform for them and so they scorn your very presence. I think I understand their evil hearts, my Lord. How often I have disdained your presence for something more tangible, something to satiate my senses, rather than sear my soul. This is how I mock you, dearest Savior—forgive me. . . . Forgive my foolish squandering of your precious grace.

CHAPTER FOUR
THE SENTENCING

Therefore, He had to be made like His brethren in all things, so that
He might become a merciful and faithful high priest in things
pertaining to God, to make propitiation for the sins of the people. For
since He Himself was tempted in that which He has suffered, He is
able to come to the aid of those who are tempted.

Hebrews 2:17–18

The letter from friends serving as missionaries across the globe left me in a somber mood. After sharing news of their family, they wrote:

> A Muslim convert, very recently baptized, was abducted by a group of leaders from the local mosque. They tried to get him to recant, to tell who the leader of the convert group was, deny his new faith, and so on. When he didn't, they cut off his fingers. He still didn't recant, so they cut off his wrists and left him outside in the cold January. He died that night. He was twenty-three.

Images from my grandfather's *Foxe's Book of Martyrs*, the pictures of which I perused as a child, came back to me as I clutched the letter. I have never been able to forget those drawings of saints being burned at the stake, boiled in oil, or hung in a basket amidst wasp nests and stung to death.

I wept for young men like this one and others who this very day face

torture and/or death for their faith in Christ. As I grieved, God called me back to the Cross.

For days I had scrutinized the suffering of Christ leading up to Calvary, pondering the events, asking: Why did the Lord suffer so? Why didn't He die quickly—why the mocking, the torture, the flogging, the spitting, and the beating? I know my salvation was purchased with His blood shed on Calvary, but what of His other wounds? What did they accomplish?

The verse from Hebrews took on new meaning as I reflected on the plight of that young man: *He had to be made like His brethren in all things*. God, in His omniscience understood that a Stephen would soon be stoned, a Paul repeatedly beaten and imprisoned, and a John exiled for life from those he loved.

He knew that in every generation to come, His followers would face the most vile kinds of torture for their faith. In order to identify with the suffering of saints throughout Christian history, Jesus could not simply march to Calvary and be executed. *He had to be made like His brethren in all things*.

In countries where religious freedom thrives, we cannot relate to our brothers and sisters whose hands are cut off in the night. It is a far and distant thing. And therefore, tragically, we have little appreciation for the horrific suffering our Lord faced, not only on the cross, but in the hours leading up to it.

But for those who are persecuted in Christ's name, these things offer sweet sustenance. They rejoice that He has walked this path before them and if their affliction leads to death, Christ, nail-scarred hands outstretched, will welcome them into glory.

How do the rest of us learn to share in the fellowship of Christ's sufferings if the circumstances of our faith don't compel us to look at them? If His journey to Golgotha is the example Jesus leaves for us to follow, how do we, whose struggles are mild by comparison, conform to it?

Our best hope of embracing the impact of Christ's passion is to accom-

pany Him often to the Cross, contemplating the wounds he bore that He might *be made like His brethren in all things*.

As we come now to the time of sentencing, these wounds multiply. We will hear His innocence proclaimed by a heathen governor, yet hear cries of *Crucify Him! Crucify Him!* from religious leaders. Drawn to reach out and comfort our Lord, we might feel the imprint of thorns on His brow, run our hands across the trenches engraved by whips on His back, or tenderly touch the bruises on His swollen face.

In this we will find we can no longer take lightly the moments of His passion. In this we may more completely identify with the one who was *made like His brethren in all things*. In this, our love for our Lord and our commitment to take up our own cross may find a home in the deepest place of our soul.

14. ABSOLVED

The very existence of the cross, and of the crucified Christ, forces us to
make a crucial decision: Will we look for God somewhere else,
or will we make the cross, and the crucified Christ,
the basis of our thought about God?

Alistair E. McGrath

Reflect

Quietly read Psalm 121 back to the Lord as a prayer. (e.g., *My help comes from you, Lord, who made heaven and earth. You will not allow my foot to slip. . . .*) Allow your mind to reflect on the truths about God that you affirm in prayer according to this Psalm.

Seek to focus solely on God who meets you here, asking Him to remove mental distractions. Ask Him to write His word for you from the cross on your heart this day.

Read

Matthew 27:15–21 and the following narrative.

But they cried out all together, saying,
"Away with this man, and release for us Barabbas!"

Luke 23:18

Back at the Praetorium, they push Jesus up some steps to a platform where the growing crowd can see him plainly. The oddity of this commoner with bruised and lacerated face wearing an expensive royal robe sets tongues wagging. Summoning the high priests and other leaders to the front, Pilate holds up his right hand to silence the crowd.

"You brought this man to me at dawn, accusing him of inciting people against the government. I have listened to all you say, I have questioned the prisoner myself, and I find him innocent of these charges. Herod agrees and has sent him back to me. Therefore, I will have him scourged and released."

Confident that this compromise will appease the priests, Pilate turns away, but is distracted by increasingly loud shouts nearby. He notices a group of well-known freedom fighters trying to get his attention.

One of his men leans over to explain that the men showed up a while ago, requesting he release their leader, Barabbas, following the custom of the Roman government to release a Jewish prisoner every Passover as a sign of peace.

To Pilate, it seems the gods have smiled upon him. Of course—this is what he can do with the innocent Galilean—let him go and be done with it. Surely, given the choice, any God-fearing Jew would prefer Jesus' release to that of the murderer Barabbas.

Ignoring the defiant revolutionaries, Pilate calls out to the high priests: "What if I give you the king of the Jews? Would you like me to release him?"

Any answer they might give is drowned out by the cries of Barabbas' friends for his emancipation. Tempers flare as the morning sun beats down its relentless heat. As Pilate observes the growing unease, a breathless messenger runs up the steps, handing him a sealed envelope.

Inside is a hastily scribbled note from his wife. *Have nothing to do with the carpenter from Nazareth. Last night I had a terrible dream about him and I have already suffered much today because of it.*

Pilate glances up to see the crowd scrutinizing his every move. The priests and other religious leaders have dispersed among them, championing their cause, stirring up the people.

Wanting to be done with it all, Pilate thunders, "Tell me now—which of the two men shall I release to you?"

In unison, it seems, every person there shouts, "Barabbas!"

Pilate stares at Jesus, who silently watches the crowd. A sadness covers his bruised face, his weary body slightly bent. It is a pitiful sight. What does he see in the agitated mob?

What must he feel as he watches the freedom fighters demand their leader's release? Their loyalty is fierce and fearless. Where are the men who promised they'd never leave *him*, never deny *him*, follow *him* to death if need be? These renegades battle brazenly for political liberation—who will carry on *his* revolution to liberate the souls of men?

Pilate ponders how to handle the innocent man who has created such a furor among the Jews. The crowd is crazy now—how easily this whole mess could ruin his reputation in Rome as a powerful leader. What in the world should he do?

"Take him and scourge him!" he barks at the soldiers, while the crowd looks on.

They drag Jesus away, every eye watching, wondering if the weakened

prisoner can possibly survive the horrific flogging to come. Pilate follows along, weary with the whole thing.

Can it still be morning? The day seems unbearably long to priests and procurators, but for the Man of Sorrows, it has only begun.

Respond

Consider the moment when the crowd called for the release of Barabbas. He was guilty of everything Jesus had been accused of—seeking political power, creating an insurgency against the government—murder and robbery and more. In the end, he will be set free.

See yourself as Barabbas, sitting in a dark cave awaiting your sentence of death. Feel your own guilt. Experience the shame of failure, the fear of eternity in darkness. Then consider how it feels to have someone open the gate, loosen your bonds, and set you free, no questions asked.

Barabbas was freed when Jesus should have been. Through Jesus' death, you are set free. Relish the reality of this and the price He paid. Feel the joy of freedom. Thank God, pour out your gratefulness to Him. Write Romans 7:24–25 as a prayer of thanksgiving to God in your prayer journal.

A Prayer

I am that prisoner, Lord, that deserves to die. I have committed crime after crime against the living God and I have no one to demand my release. No one except you. How can I ever comprehend that at this very moment you stand before the Father doing just that? Praying for me? How will I ever grasp the mystery that you went to your death, innocent of every charge, while I am free today? Incomprehensible—these things are inexplicable to me.

15. SCOURGED

Of all the pains that lead to salvation this is the most pain, to see Thy
Love suffer. How might any pain be more to me than to see Him
that is all my life, all my bliss, and all my joy suffer?

Julian of Norwich

Reflect

Today we will look at the scourging of Jesus. It will be difficult, painful, perhaps even nauseating. Spend enough time in God's presence to prepare your heart. Sing to yourself, *Jesus loves me, this I know.*

Read Philippians 3:10. Say the words, phrase by phrase, slowly, considering what each one means. The word "fellowship" here refers almost to a sense of partnership. Offer yourself to walk in communion through these sufferings of the Lord, asking Him to reveal himself to you in a fresh way today.

Read

John 19:1 and the following narrative.[1]

The chastening for our well-being fell upon Him,
and by His scourging we are healed.

Isaiah 53:5

Inside the palace courtyard soldiers prepare for the scourging, paying little attention to Jesus. With businesslike precision one rips the robe from his shoulders, and another removes the rest of his clothes. A grim-faced Jesus offers no resistance.

Exposed . . . vulnerable . . . defenseless in every way. Does he commune in spirit with his Father as the morning air assaults his naked body? Is this part of the cup he cried out against in the Garden only hours ago?

Roughly they drag him to a column stained with layer after layer of blood. Pushing him to his knees, they lift his arms above his head, securing them to the post. A soldier stands to his right and another to his left, awaiting the order to begin. Does Jesus see frail sinners in need of a Savior behind their hardened eyes?

Each holds a vicious looking whip, several feet long. Halfway down it is split into numerous leather strips to which pieces of sheep bone are attached. Two lead balls hang at the end of every strip.

Jesus knows a brief moment of cool relief as he rests his cheek against the column.

"Begin!" The command is given.

The soldier on the right, well trained and competent from years of experience with the flagellum, strikes the first blow. A crack resounds throughout the courtyard, spilling over into the silent wake of those who wait outside.

At first, the bones make tiny cuts on Jesus' back, the iron balls raising red welts that quickly turn to purple bruises. With each blow, Jesus' body recoils. Just as he catches his breath, clutching the column for strength, another strike is administered.

Crack.

Silence.

Crack.

Silence.

And on and on it goes until the first soldier tires. The second steps in quickly, not missing a beat. By now the small cuts are bleeding profusely, and a few of the large bruises are breaking open.

Jesus' strength fails, the loss of blood making him lightheaded and dizzy.

He winces now only slightly with each lash of the whip.

Crack.

Silence.

Crack.

Silence.

The blood gushes from several places. Soldiers turn away, feigning busyness to avoid the horrid sight of gaping wounds. Tiny ribbons of flesh are all that remain on Jesus' back.

The officer is just doing a job—one he's done a thousand times before. But does he have any idea to whom he inflicts such hideous blows?

Crack.

Silence.

Crack.

Silence.

Crack.

The two soldiers take their turns, oblivious to the condition of the prisoner until Pilate calls a halt to the bloody operation. The victim has not moved for several minutes now. If he dies here, they will all face grave reprimands and the loss of their esteemed position in the royal army.

Quickly they move to untie him. Flanking him on either side, soldiers lift the near unconscious prisoner to his feet. Jesus manages to open his eyes briefly and somehow finds the fortitude to stand. Searing pain slices through him as they put clothes back on his battered body.

Then he is led out to the platform. The crowd waits in anticipation for the grand finale of their morning merrymaking. Soldiers on either side secure his feet and gingerly step away. Somehow he manages not to collapse. Pilate, frustrated and frightened because of his wife's dream, looks at the beaten down would-be king.

Rancor resonates in his curt challenge to the crowd: *Behold the man!*

And demons celebrate. The Father hangs His head and weeps, for

though He could heal the mass of bleeding tissue with a word, He won't. The words of the prophet Isaiah play a haunting melody through the halls of heaven. Today the Son of God is bruised for the iniquities of a dying world, and by his stripes, humanity can finally be healed.

Respond

Take some time to contemplate the moments of scourging Christ endured. As you form this picture in your mind, read aloud Isaiah 53:4–6. In every bruise that each ball of lead inflicted, see your personal sin. With each bloody cut the leather and bone made, see the healing you have come to know in Him. Speak verse six in your own words. Take the time to mourn over this. Write it out as a prayer of worship.

Receive forgiveness and healing, rejoicing (perhaps in a bittersweet way) that Jesus did this for you.

A Prayer

Must I go on, Lord Jesus? I can barely stand to see myself through the gaping wounds on your back. My stomach churns and I want to walk away. The journey to the Cross is fraught with a thousand deaths and I'm not sure if I am prepared to embrace each one. To know the fellowship of your sufferings is not so simple. Sustain me in my quest, dearest Savior, and I will seek to share your sorrow.

16. FINAL QUESTIONING

Where have your love, your mercy, your compassion shone out more luminously than in your wounds, sweet gentle Lord of mercy? More mercy than this no one has than that he lay down his life for those who are doomed to death.

Bernard of Clairvaux

Reflect

Has the Cross become a place of familiar consolation to you yet? Are you beginning to feel a drawing in your soul to reflect often on the sorrows of Calvary? Take a few minutes as you quiet your heart to consider what the Cross of Christ means to you after reflecting on it through the past days or weeks. Offer words of thanksgiving to Jesus for the specific ways His Cross touches you.

Read or sing the words to the following hymn, contemplating the depth of each phrase.

Beneath the Cross of Jesus
Elizabeth C. Clephane

Beneath the cross of Jesus
I fain would take my stand.
The shadow of a mighty Rock
Within a weary land.
A home within the wilderness,
A rest upon the way
From the burning of the noonday heat
And the burden of the day.

Upon that cross of Jesus
Mine eye at times can see
The very dying form of One
Who suffered there for me.
And from my smitten heart with tears
Two wonders I confess—
The wonders of His glorious love
And my unworthiness.

I take, O cross, thy shadow
For my abiding place—
I ask no other sunshine than
The sunshine of His face;
Content to let the world go by,
To know no gain nor loss,
My sinful self my only shame,
My glory all the cross.

Read

John 19:6–11 and the following narrative.

But they shouted all the more, "Crucify Him!"

Mark 15:14

The battered prisoner barely stands, a solemn symbol of Rome's power to destroy. Wanting to get away from it all, and confident the extremely brutal beating will satisfy the Jewish priests, Pilate asks once again: "Then what shall I do with Jesus who is called the Christ?"

Before the words are out of his mouth a loud cry ensues: "Crucify, crucify!"

"Me? But I believe he's innocent. Tell me, what evil has he done? Take him yourselves and crucify him. I find no guilt in him."

Pilate knows his offer is an empty one, for the power to execute lies with him alone. Try as he might, he cannot get this man's future out of his own hands.

Jesus struggles to keep his balance. He has lost so much blood, his head at times seems to float above him. Standing here, he is the only one who

really knows the end of this story. Does he wish he could just speak and be on his way to Golgotha? If this entire crowd suddenly stopped to listen to *him*, what would he say?

"He says he is the Son of God, and by our laws, for this he must die." A high priest makes his voice heard above the crowd.

Superstitious fear grips Pilate upon hearing these words. Son of God? He hasn't heard this charge before. Is this why his wife warned him to steer clear of this man? Does he have mystical powers? Watching the broken prisoner, it seems nothing could be further from the truth.

Turning quickly, Pilate motions for them to bring Jesus back into the palace. He must get to the bottom of this.

"Where do you come from?" Knowing the answer already, Pilate gives the prisoner a chance to deny their charges of a claim to deity.

Jesus looks at him but says nothing.

"Why won't you talk to me?" Pilate pleads, baffled again by this one who offers no self-defense. It is unheard of—he must be crazy.

"Don't you understand that I have the power here, that with a word I can release you *or* crucify you?"

Looking off as if in a trance, Jesus smiles slightly. Is he moving through the caverns of his eternal memory to the time when the lamb was slain from the foundation of the world? Does he see the moment before his incarnation, when he offered himself to redeem mankind? Does he recall his agony of a few hours past when he made the choice to drink this very cup? What thoughts drive him to finally respond to Pilate?

"You have no power over me, except that which is given to you from above. The one who turned me over to you has the greater sin here."

Pilate bristles at the affront to his authority, but senses a strange relief. He has done all he can do. He looks once more into the eyes of the Christ, frustrated at his failure to figure this odd prisoner out. Shaking his head, he walks back onto the platform, leaving him behind with the guards.

Distant cries for execution tick like a time bomb in Jesus' ear. But perhaps he garners a measure of strength in the words of truth he has just spoken. For though he feels his wounds in every excruciating move of his body, no one can take his life from him—he alone has the power to give it.

Faces flash across his mind—fishermen, priests, prostitutes, mothers, children, tax collectors, doctors, friends, and enemies. In every countenance he sees the desperate need for a redeemer. For these he came . . . for these he presses on.

Respond

Examine the weariness Jesus must have felt as He was constantly passed from one person to another. He allowed himself to be completely at their mercy. Physically He must have been in torment. Take a few minutes to contemplate the physical and emotional state of Jesus at this time.

On many previous occasions, Jesus could have been arrested or killed, but He escaped (see John 8:59; 10:39). Reflect on the reality that every moment of this experience is not only preordained by the Father but chosen by the Son.

Read John 17:1–2. To glorify means to confer honor, praise, to magnify. Jesus seems to be saying that the Cross is an honor to Him. Consider this in light of His suffering. Consider this in light of His motivation in verse two—to give you eternal life. Write a prayer in which you glorify Christ—give Him the honor, praise, and worship due Him as He faces the Cross.

A Prayer

Do you call this glory, my Lord? I will never comprehend this thing—that you considered the Cross an honor when you could have commanded all heaven and earth to bow down before you. But though you despised the shame of it all, you were honored to suffer that I might know you. I cannot grasp this Lord—give me discernment in my heart of hearts.

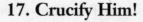

17. Crucify Him!

And, unfortunately, it is certain that I am also one of that crowd that doesn't give much thought to what happened. I, who am even able to write these things about the Passion while remaining impassive, whereas it should only be written about in tears.

Raneiro Cantallamesa

Reflect

Take the time to silence other sounds today—unplug the phone, turn off the radio, TV, CD player, put a sign on your door: DO NOT DISTURB. In silence, be still and know that God speaks to you. Thank Him for meeting you here day after day without fail.

Ask God to reveal to you the true condition of your heart. Read these verses slowly and thoughtfully, letting God open your eyes as you reevaluate: Psalm 36:1–2; 1 John 1:8; Revelation 3:17.

Do you see yourself as wretched, poor, needy, full of sin? It is important to see yourself in this way in order to fully appreciate Christ's death for you. Write a prayer of commitment to seek this kind of heart, based on these verses.

Read

John 19:12–15; Matthew 27:24–25; and the following narrative.

And all the people answered and said,
"His blood be on us and on our children!"

Matthew 27:25

When Pilate appears on the Praetorium platform alone, the clamorous crowd objects. By now many hunger for the excitement of an execution. The priests and elders have done an admirable job of portraying the prisoner as vile and dangerous, a threat to their rigid faith.

"If you let him go, you are no friend of Caesar's."

"He calls himself a king. That makes him an enemy of Caesar!"

Pilate listens in amazement at the Jews' loyalty to the Roman conqueror. How fickle they are and how intent on destroying this Jesus. Nevertheless, their threat must be taken seriously. If word reaches Tiberius that Pilate is befriending an insurrectionist, his personal and political future will be in grave danger. Shaking his head, he turns away.

In a few minutes he comes back out, this time with the prisoner. Jesus stumbles forward. Herod's robe has disappeared, and wounds ooze through his clothes, though the blood has hardened in places, binding his tunic to his back. His face, bloated and bruised, looks pasty white, his eyes nearly swollen shut.

Is he so gripped with pain that the noisy chatter from below drifts in and out of his consciousness? Does he ache for a seraph to come and cool his brow or bind his wounds? Judgment is nigh for the one who will one day judge the world. What does he think of his accusers, who've also become judge and jury to this case? What does he see in the procurator who persists in proclaiming his innocence?

Taking his official seat on the platform, Pilate motions for the soldiers to bring Jesus forward. From here he will pass sentence. The late morning sun beats down and a servant rushes to hold an umbrella over Pilate's head. No shade is offered the prisoner who now leans against a soldier's arm.

"Here is your king!" Pilate taunts the religious leaders.

"Take him away. Crucify him!" they cry back.

"What? Shall I crucify your king?"

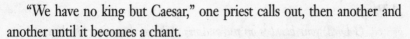

"We have no king but Caesar," one priest calls out, then another and another until it becomes a chant.

Pilate, astonished at their fervor, motions to a guard. The noise dies down as he sets a basin of water before Pilate. Slowly and methodically the procurator rinses his hands in it. Looking up, he calls out: "I am innocent of the blood of this righteous man. See to it yourselves."

His blood shall be on us and on our children! a high priest calls out. Once again others join in until the words become a chant. According to sacred law, when someone is found guilty, the accusers must take moral responsibility for the punishment. In this case, the religious leaders relish the idea, and the chant grows louder.

His blood shall be on us and on our children! It slices through the air like another blow assaulting Jesus the Christ. These whose duty it is to lead their people to God, cannot comprehend the significance of their own words.

For it is not this sham of a trial that sends Jesus to Calvary, but a people who've fallen short of God's glory. No one can wash their hands of him, but the blood he sheds there fills a fountain where all may plunge, losing their guilty stains. His blood is on us all—it has the power to heal an eternity of hell within the hearts of mankind.

Respond

Hear the words as a chant in your own ears: "His blood shall be on us and on our children." What must Jesus have heard in those words? What might He have wanted to say? Say to Him now, "Jesus, your blood be on me—I take responsibility for your death—your blood be on me." Examine this concept.

Read Psalm 36:5–9 aloud as a prayer of worship and gratitude that you can come to the healing waters of Christ's shed blood today and every day.

A Prayer

O Lord, your blood is on me and my children. I say it with shame. I cannot even look into your eyes, for the sadness there reopens the wounds of my sinful heart, and like an infected sore, they ooze with sordid filth. But I must look—I must, for through the sorrow you invite me to come and to be cleansed. And so I will—let your blood be on me, and in me and over me until I am pure, precious Redeemer.

18. SENTENCED

Thorns, it seems, always accompany visits to glory. No one who has walked in Christ's presence will ever be allowed to strut.

Jamie Buckingham

Reflect

Rejoice today that God is here. Turn your thoughts toward Him, asking that He reveal himself to you in a unique way through this time with Him.

Read Isaiah 52:14. This prophesy is fulfilled in the passage we will contemplate today. Read the words to the following old hymn meditatively.

O Sacred Head, Now Wounded
Bernard of Clairvaux

O sacred Head, now wounded,
With grief and shame weighed down,
Now scornfully surrounded
With thorns Thy only crown.
O sacred head, no glory now
From your face does shine;
Yet, though despised and gory,
I joy to call you mine.

Men mock and taunt and jeer you.
They smite your countenance.
Though mighty worlds shall fear you
And flee before your glance.
How pale you are with anguish,
With sore abuse and scorn!
Your eyes with pain now languish
That once were bright as morn!

My burden in your passion,
Lord, you have borne for me,
For it was my transgression,
My shame, on Calvary.
I cast me down before you;
Wrath is my rightful lot.
Have mercy, I implore you;
Redeemer, spurn me not!

What language shall I borrow
To thank you, dearest Friend,
For this, your dying sorrow,
Your pity without end?
O make me yours forever,
And keep me strong and true;
Lord, let me never, never
Outlive my love for you.

Now offer the words to the Lord as a prayer—either sing them or read them.

Read

John 19:16; Matthew 27:27–30; and the following narrative.

And they began to acclaim Him, "Hail, King of the Jews!"

Mark 15:18

Pilate watches the crowd with contempt and fear. How he deplores giving them their way. But what else can he do? God knows he has tried to release this eccentric Jew. There are simply no more options. He summons a centurion, mouthing terse orders.

The priests and elders continue to cry out loudly for crucifixion. Jesus sways to one side. He appears to be on the verge of passing out.

The centurion returns holding the arm of Barabbas. Pilate declares his official release and the crowd cheers as Barabbas joins his fellow revolutionaries below. Meanwhile, the soldiers flanking Jesus pull him along to the palace courtyard. Breathing a collective sigh of relief, the priests and elders are confident that execution is inevitable.

The crowd begins to break up. Some head to the temple for worship, while others move to the marketplace to buy unleavened bread for the day's meal. Many remain, waiting for the prisoner to be led out to the place called Golgotha.

Inside the courtyard, soldiers form rows of military precision in preparation for the imminent death march. What a pitiful sight is the capital offender—one more crazy Jew with a messiah complex. How could this one ever make any claim to royalty? What would make him dream such dreams?

A few joke at the absurdity of the whole thing. One grabs a thin branch covered with long hard thorns from a pile of firewood nearby, and begins to weave it into a wreath to crown the would-be king.

Seeing them, a captain from the Italian regiment takes off his military robe. With dramatic flare, he drapes it across Jesus' shoulders, bowing deeply

as he backs away. One by one others pick up the revelry, laughing and taunting the Christ. Finished with his crown, the soldier places it on Jesus' head, mimicking an official coronation.

"Hail, King of the Jews!" he cries out jovially. Others crowd around, fawning over Jesus as they drop to their knees and salute with words of cheer.

"Godspeed, O mighty one!"

"Rejoice, O great ruler!"

"Hail, King of the Jews!"

A centurion calls out: "His scepter—he is a king, he must have a scepter!" Someone grabs one of the branches from the pile and places it in Jesus' right hand.

He is so very alone now. What must he feel in this crowd? At least his own people, though they knew him not, expectantly awaited the Messiah foretold in sacred Scripture. Whether they loved or hated him, Jesus' claims were always taken seriously.

But these Gentiles—have they ever wanted a savior? Or does the power they hold rob them of any sense of their need? When Jesus looks at them, does he see the frailty behind their pride? In the mocking faces, does he see some who will one day follow him? Does he gaze into the eyes of a Cornelius and secretly rejoice at what he will be, once the price has been paid for his sins?

The blood drips down into his eyes and across his face, the makeshift crown slipping from his matted hair. Someone grabs a branch and hits at it, embedding the barbs in his skull. A vicious lust for blood spurs soldier after soldier to join in pounding Jesus' head with reeds.

One squares off, slaps him, and spits in his face. A few others follow suit. The fun and games have become a sadistic sport, with Jesus the impotent victim.

Crowned with thorns, the King of kings finally faces death's mournful march. Eternal darkness looms over the One to whom every eye will one

day look, though for now his battered face is repulsive to see. Weak and powerless, the Mighty Warrior advances toward a host of hell's demons to wage the final war for the souls of men.

Respond

The walk to Golgotha is almost here. Consider the emotions Jesus must face at this moment. Think of His physical state. Contemplate the mockery that He faced from the Romans. See this scene before you as you read Revelation 4:2–11. Consider the contrast. Reflect on what Jesus endured in light of what He could have clung to.

Write a prayer of adoration based on these thoughts. Spend some time in quiet contemplation of these things.

A Prayer

O my Lord of lords—you whose head should bear only crowns of gold are wreathed with nasty thorns. You who should be hailed as matchless King are ridiculed with words of salutation. You whose heavenly anthem should drown all other sounds are deluged with derisive taunts. Every melody of love loses its luster in light of this haunting song you sing. How can we ever join the chorus, except with tears?

Notes

1. Because I have sought to include details from all four Gospel accounts, I show Jesus scourged in the middle of the trial (John's account), and mocked at the end (Matthew and Mark).

CHAPTER FIVE
CALVARY

For it was fitting for Him, for whom are all things, and through whom are all things, in bringing many sons to glory, to perfect the author of their salvation through sufferings.

Hebrews 2:10

I heard it again this Easter—a radio preacher proclaiming with great fervor that *our* God doesn't hang from a cross. He is risen! It's a familiar message, one which characterized my evangelical upbringing. We didn't ignore the death of Christ, but Easter was the central holiday of our faith. Somehow the Crucifixion paled in significance to the Resurrection.

Until my adult years I had never heard of a Good Friday service. My conservative Christian church celebrated Communion once a month on a Sunday night when the crowds were low. My strongest memory of those services isn't the sufferings of Christ, but the controversy over who should be allowed to take the crackers and grape juice.

I think of it now and grieve. There is great disparity between Scripture and Christian dogma that elevates the Resurrection above the Cross of Jesus Christ. It is true, as I often heard taught, that without the Resurrection the Cross would have accomplished nothing, and we would still be powerless over sin. But it is equally true, that without the shedding of blood, there *is no* remission of sin (Hebrews 9:22).

97

Jesus lived His life with penetrating awareness of His impending death. He described it in detail to His disciples three times and alluded to it on eight other occasions. He used His final meal with them to graphically illustrate the reality of His spilled blood and broken body.

The disciples who wrote of Jesus' life spent more time detailing his death than anything else. John devotes almost half his story to Jesus' final hours. The apostle Paul championed a crucified Christ, boldly making this the centerpiece of his faith. Peter tells us that not only Christ's death but the way He died is the supreme example of how we are to live on earth (1 Peter 2:21–24).

Our clearest picture of eternity is the revelation given to John on the Isle of Patmos. There, *the Lamb that was slain* opens the book of life and receives worship from heavenly hosts and redeemed saints from every tribe, tongue, and nation. Twenty-seven times Christ is referred to as the *Lamb* in John's vision. The *Lamb* is on the throne to receive blessing and glory and wisdom and thanksgiving and honor and power and might forever and ever. Amen (Revelation 7:12).

I cherish Easter celebrations. In them we embrace our victory in Christ, power over the forces of darkness, and the hope implanted within us through the Holy Spirit. But I don't want to rush past the Cross to get there. The depth of my appreciation for those glorious truths will be directly related to my comprehension of Christ's bloody battle for my sins on Calvary.

At the very heart of our faith is a God who aches to share His love with His children, a God who gave His own life for our sakes. How precious the reality of the Cross must become to us. It's message must shake us, its essence shape us, and its reality consume us until we cry out like Paul: "May it never be that I would boast, except in the cross of our Lord Jesus Christ . . ." (Galatians 6:14).

19. LED AWAY

At the head of the procession of life, then, is a thorn-crowned Man,
his pains healing our pains, his wounds answering our wounds,
his love taking our sin.

Earl Stanley Jones

Reflect

Today the walk up Calvary begins, and it is important to prepare for God's voice. Contemplating the Cross can be an emotional, spiritual, and even physical experience. Ask God to help you focus, letting other cares dissipate in light of the love you will see. Be quiet in His presence for a few minutes.

Read the following prayer (taken from *The Book of Common Worship*, Presbyterian Church), offering each phrase from your own heart to the Lord for this time of contemplation.

> *Forbid, O God, that we should forget, amid our earthly comforts, the pains and mortal anguish that our Lord Jesus endured for our salvation. Grant us this day a true vision of all that He suffered, in His betrayal, His lonely agony, His false trial, His mocking and scourging, and the torture of death upon the cross. As Thou hast given Thyself utterly for us, may we give ourselves entirely to Thee, O Jesus Christ, our only Lord and Savior. Amen.*

Read

Matthew 27:31 and the following narrative.

And they led Him out to crucify Him.

Mark 15:20

A hush falls over the courtyard as Pilate enters with his entourage. The prisoner, sickly and silent, stares at the ground. Blood covers his face from the thorny wreath and several large lumps have appeared where the soldiers hit him with reeds. Pilate shakes his head in disgust.

Angrily he shouts orders to bring out the other prisoners and prepare all three for crucifixion. Two men strip Jesus of the cloak he wore while they mocked him. He winces with each touch of their hands.

Three soldiers enter the courtyard, each carrying a wooden plank. Weighing almost 100 pounds and measuring six feet long, the beams are an ominous reminder that Rome's most grueling form of execution will soon take place.

Can Jesus even lift his head? The effects of the scourging could claim his life here in the courtyard. Does he fight such an outcome? Does the Divine captive cling to his humanity in order to hang from a cross, paying the full price to purchase souls enslaved by sin?

Holding his hands in front of him, they place the heavy beam across Jesus' left shoulder. One at a time they tie each wrist to the wood, so he will be able to drag it without dropping it. The massive weight against the open wounds on his back cause him to hunch over in anguish. As he struggles to stand straight, the rough wood rubs against his raw flesh, planting splinters in his arms. How much more can one body take?

The centurion in charge of executions motions to the soldiers. Jesus, pushed to the front and flanked on all sides by officers of the Roman army, moves through the arches of the palace courtyard and into the street. Several

priests and elders wait to accompany the procession. Families line the narrow road that will take the prisoner away from town to the foot of Golgotha.

Jesus' eyes blink in the glaring sun as he tries to survey the streets of Jerusalem one last time. In the marketplace, men and women conduct the business of life, and boys and girls play merrily as if it were any other day. The journey to Calvary, which began in the heart of his Father before the earth was formed, now has only 650 yards to go. Yet for this one whose broken body screams in pain with every step, it spans an eternity of torment whose end cannot even be fathomed.

Respond

Sit very still, listening to the sounds of Jerusalem—the busy marketplace, the hustle and bustle of ordinary life. Hear the sounds of your own world today—phones, traffic, radios, TV, talking, laughing, etc. Now, in your mind, freeze frame these two scenes side by side. In the middle of them, see Jesus, beaten, barely able to move, bent under the weight of the crossbeam. Sense the significance of a world that goes on, oblivious to the reality of a living Sacrifice being led to the slaughter on their behalf.

Consider the days of your own life when you are unaware, insensitive to Christ's journey to the Cross, to the extreme price He paid for you . . . for you. Contemplate the kind of love that keeps on giving, even in the face of such apathy. Respond with worship, tears, repentance, rejoicing—whatever God places in your heart.

Write a prayer beginning with these words: *Lord Jesus, you walk today and every day to Calvary, while I . . .*

A Prayer

Lord Jesus, you walk today and every day to Calvary, while I make beds and drive carpools. You bleed, wounds festering, body failing, while I pay bills and play tennis. You trudge along, one lonely step after another,

while I make phone calls and go shopping. Lord Jesus, you walk today and every day to Calvary for me—grant that this thought will crash through my callous oblivion, piercing my busyness with pangs of brokenhearted love.

20. VIA DOLOROSA

When we look at his cross, we understand his love. His head is bent down to kiss us. His hands are extended to embrace us. His heart is wide open to receive us.

Mother Teresa

Reflect

Come in deep reverence to spend time in God's presence today. Gently open your heart—see yourself taking off your shoes to enter the Holy of Holies where God will speak to your own heart.

Read Colossians 1:15–17 as a prayer back to Christ (i.e., *You are the image of the invisible God, the firstborn of* . . .). Write it in your prayer journal. Hold this reality close as you encounter this same Jesus on the *Via Dolorosa*—the way of suffering—today.

Read

Luke 23:26–32 and the following narrative.

They took Jesus, therefore, and He went out, bearing His own cross.

John 19:17

Because the number of Jews in the city swells by tens of thousands during Passover, conducting crucifixions is not an easy task. The road is narrow, and the soldiers have their hands full clearing the streets for the procession. Jesus grimaces with each step. The other two prisoners are pushed ahead for they are stronger than this one who's been scourged.

Every couple of feet Jesus stops, unable to go on. His feet ache from the rocks strewn along the path, and he can hardly catch his breath through the pain that now permeates his entire body. Fever infuses his flesh. He lurches forward. Dazed and almost delirious, the broken prisoner finally collapses face down in the dirt.

Arms askew, the crossbeam lands heavily on his shoulders, pinning him to the ground. To those whose curiosity compels them to watch the pitiful scene, it appears he may have died. Word passes up the line and the centurion halts the procession. Hurrying back to the place where Jesus lays, he surveys the crowd.

"You, there—yes, you. Come here."

Simon, a large man from Cyrene in North Africa, steps back, hoping they don't mean him. Having just come in from the country to take his sons to the temple, he tries to turn and be on his way.

"You, I said, you—come take this stake and carry it to Golgotha."

With these words an ordinary father, a preoccupied pilgrim is pressed into service for the Savior of the world. Does rage at Rome's intrusion on his life burn within? Does he feel for his fellow Jew who's been treated so cruelly? Does he have any idea how this single event will impact history? Will Passover ever be the same for Simon the Cyrenian?

Soldiers untie the beam from Jesus' wrists and pass it to Simon. Fearful that the prisoner will die before the official execution, the captain of the guard leans down to pull Jesus gently to his feet. Staggering, he opens his eyes.

A distant sound breaks through the stillness that has surrounded the

scene at Jerusalem's gates. As the procession moves out, it gets louder. The earsplitting noise is chilling—women with no self-control, weeping and wailing for the one who cannot carry his own cross.

Who are these women? Professional mourners, given the task of lamenting the death of any and all who face crucifixion? Women whose husbands once left them behind to join the radical rabbi's movement? Friends of the victim's mother, Mary? Or women who perhaps not long ago found compassion in the eyes of this one now condemned by envious elders?

Stopping, Jesus peers into the faces of the mourners. A tear slips from one blue-black eye. From deep within he summons a strange stamina and speaks with the authority of a prophet.

"Daughters of Jerusalem, don't weep for me. Weep for yourselves and for your children."

The crowd is hushed, tearstained faces bewildered at Jesus' sudden burst of energy. He continues.

"A time is coming when you will believe that it is a blessed thing to be barren, to never have had children in this evil world."

The women murmur among themselves. What is he saying? Empty wombs are the curse of Jewish women. How could that ever be a blessing?

Scanning the faces in the crowd, Jesus goes on. "You will beg the mountains to fall and crush you and the hills to cover you completely. For if these things happen to a green tree, what will happen to those that are dry?"

Even in the throes of agony, Jesus longs to warn men and women of the wrath to come. What kind of yearning fills his heart? Does he see those who will reject his offer of salvation, even after he has paid such a price? Does he fret for those who mourn now, but will never truly repent? In this moment, does he intercede on behalf of these to the Father?

Soldiers weave through the crowd, breaking it up as they press the prisoner forward. What an odd man this is. A few seconds ago, battered almost to the point of death, he collapsed under his own crossbeam. Now he stands

strong, admonishing the crowd with words none of them seem to understand.

And the march moves on. Jesus, who for one brief moment forgot his pain, struggles again with each step. They pass through a nondescript neighborhood where people declare him guilty or innocent from their rooftops. Pharisees with their phylacteries containing the sacred words of Scripture flank the procession on either side. And the living Word of God moves outside the gate of the city, with only a hill left to climb.

Respond

Place yourself in the street of Jerusalem that day. When Jesus falls, would you gladly carry His cross? Would your heart break with the women? What would you do as He passes by? Wipe His face with a cool cloth? Offer Him a drink of pure water? Look into His pain-wracked eyes and tell Him you are sorry He suffers so?

Spend some time contemplating this, then offer your response to Him. Tell Him from your heart how you feel this moment and what you would do to change things if you could.

A Prayer

O God, I am a woman mourning today. I want to wail at what they have done to you, to cry gut-wrenching sobs over your mutilated back and pummeled face. I want to stop the whole thing and make it go away. I want to have never been the reason for your journey down Via Dolorosa. How foolish the thought. For I have sinned and it is the weight of this—not a wooden beam—that hurls you to the ground. I mourn, for what else can I do?

21. GOLGOTHA

*I want to recover the truth that Jesus was not crucified on an altar
between two candlesticks, but on a garbage heap at a crossroads of the
world . . . where soldiers gambled and cynics talked smut.*

George McCloud

Reflect

Sit in hushed silence with God today, enjoying Him, relishing these moments as precious gifts to you and blessings to Him. There is great sorrow in the Cross, but also great joy. The anticipation of joy is what enabled Jesus to endure the horror of Calvary. Read the following quote slowly and offer it as a prayer (or give your own) to the Lord based on the joy you sense as you consider the Cross today.

How Splendid the Cross
St. Theodore of Studios

How splendid the cross of Christ!
It brings life, not death;
light, not darkness;
Paradise, not its loss.
It is the wood on which
the Lord, like a great warrior,
was wounded in hands and feet and side,
but healed thereby our wounds.
A tree had destroyed us;
a tree now brought us life.

As quoted in *Breakfast With the Saints*

Read

Matthew 27:33–34 and the following narrative.

And they brought Him to the place Golgotha, which is translated,
Place of a Skull.

Mark 15:22

The small hill outside the Gennath Gate in Jerusalem buzzes with crucifixion activity. The other two criminals have begun their ascent and Jesus waits at the bottom, trying to muster enough strength for the short climb.

Two major roads intersect at the base of Golgotha. Merchants from the port of Joppa in the west and travelers from Samaria to the north or even further south have a clear view up the fifteen-foot slope as they enter the city.

For the Romans, this has proven an effective deterrent to crime. On any given day, a number of beams bear the bodies of the accused in the most vile and inhumane manner imaginable. Today there are three.

Soldiers shout at those crowding the busy crossroads. They must get this prisoner up the last leg of their journey before he passes out or dies. Every step Jesus takes, every movement in his body, inflicts pain beyond comprehension. Centurions on either side move him forward.

Snippets of conversation drift through the air concerning how the grassy knoll got its name. Some say the hill looks like a skull, with two caverns for eyes and a large jutting rock formation for a nose. Others believe the "Place of a Skull" refers to the thousands of criminals executed here. Whatever one's opinion, the mount outside the city gate is certainly worthy of its title. It is a symbol of death to all whose lives it touches.

Passersby hurry past the group approaching the incline, hiding their chil-

dren's eyes from the gruesome sight of the prisoner. But those who have followed since the trial at Castle Antonia jostle and push, anxious to get a good view at the foot of the three beams.

What occupies the mind of Christ as he faces the final steps to his death? Does dread eat at his resolve? Is he fraught with the kind of fear that makes your heart pound and your stomach heave? Does he long to draw on Divine resources, to make himself whole, to infuse supernatural strength throughout his broken body?

As they reach the top, a soldier orders Simon to drop the crossbeam. Another moves toward Jesus, handing him a metal cup. How thirsty he must be. Has he had so much as a sip of water since his arrest in Gethsemane? The cup must seem like a gift, a respite from the raging war within and without.

He holds it to his split and swollen lips, but barely tastes the foul potion before handing the cup back. It is sour wine mixed with myrrh, an analgesic to deaden his senses and ease the pain. The Romans prefer civilized executions, and without sedation crucified criminals often scream in agony. Never before has a prisoner refused to drink it. The soldier shrugs, tossing the brew to the ground.

Does this cup remind Jesus of the cup he cried out against only last night? That which he promised the Father he would drink? That cup is bitter too, but it cannot ease his pain, for in every swallow he will consume the filth of a sin-sick world. Does he consider that even now he could dash it to the ground like the sticky wine on the grass at his feet?

Like the bodies of sacrificial animals that priests for centuries have removed from the camp to burn, the stench of Jesus' flesh will soon waft through the air outside Jerusalem's gates. But first, the blood of the Lamb must be spilt on this altar that was fashioned before the foundation of the world.

Respond

In your own mind, stand at the top of Mount Calvary. See the crowds coming and going below. See the massive temple and the beautiful city of Jerusalem. Hear the conversations of those who've come up the hill. Watch Jesus take the final steps to the top. Imagine His emotions, thoughts, and fears.

Read Hebrews 13:11–13. See Jesus suffering outside the gate of Jerusalem. Go to Him, bearing (figuratively carrying) His reproach (suffering, reviling, upbraiding). This simply means to feel within and have a deep appreciation for all He endured, willing to suffer yourself, if it will further His kingdom.

After a while, write a few words expressing your thoughts and compassion to Christ.

A Prayer

Lord, you who own the cattle on a thousand hills now suffer reproach on one of them. The scent of your sacrifice is a stench in the nostrils of those who do not understand, those who look the other way, those who clutch their rebellion to their blackened heart. But to me, Lord, it is sweet—sometimes too strong for my sinful soul—but sweet nonetheless. Help me to breathe deeply that your aroma of death might finally permeate my heart of hearts.

22. NAILED TO THE CROSS

And if we men and women of this latter day wish to gaze into the awfulness of sin, we shall have to take our stand at the mystic confluence of midnight and noonday and abide in the Cross of our Lord Jesus Christ.

Warren Wiersbe

Reflect

Set your heart toward God today. Acknowledge His presence with you, thanking Him for His faithfulness. Ask Him to give you a tenderness toward His Son in death. Read John 12:32–33. Consider this truth in today's narrative as you focus on Jesus being lifted up to die. Stop at times while you are reading and speak this verse aloud, offering a heart of gratitude to Him.

Read

John 19:18 and the following narrative.

> *And when they came to the place called The Skull,*
> *there they crucified Him.*

Luke 23:33

The four soldiers assigned to crucify the prisoner named Jesus move quickly into action. First they strip him of his clothing. When they reach the inner garments, blood and flesh tear from wounds already festering with grisly infection. Jesus' eyes roll back in his head in agony. The crucifixion has begun.

Women turn their heads in shame at the sight of his bare body. The extent of his wounds shocks even the soldiers who take the task of execution lightly. One grabs the loincloth and begins to wrap it around Jesus' waist and through his legs. If he weren't Jewish, he would be hung naked. It is a small concession to the Jews whose sacred beliefs abhor nudity.

Then the soldiers lead Jesus to the crossbeam on the ground. They instruct him to lay down and place his arms out to his sides on the rough wood. Some prisoners won't cooperate and must be shoved to the ground, head

banging on the wood. But Jesus responds with perplexing submission.

What must it be like for the Son of God to finally lay down his life? How does it feel to stretch his arms out on the crossbeam of crucifixion? Does he embrace this moment for which he entered the human race? Can he yet see the joy of victory somewhere in the vast expanse of eternity?

His head falls back on the ground, the crown of thorns pressing deeper into his skull. Mustering his strength, he raises up level with the crossbeam. Dirt and leaves cling to the open wounds on his back and legs. One soldier holds Jesus' right arm loosely across the wood. The other positions the tip of an iron spike, five inches long and almost a half inch across, in the middle of his wrist.

An expert in the art of crucifixion, the soldier lifts his hammer and with one strike embeds the nail through the flesh into the wood. The loud pinging thud echoes across the hill as the crowd watches. Only a trickle of blood appears and the soldier knows he hasn't severed any main arteries. To do so would bring quick death, something that must not happen. The longer it takes, the greater the suffering, and the more people will see and be cowed into allegiance to the Roman government.

The spike crushes numerous nerve endings, and Jesus moans. Bolts of pain shoot down the length of his arm. Before he can catch his breath, they extend the other one. The sound of hammer against iron rings again in the ears of onlookers. Now pain radiates through both arms, up his neck, through his ears and eyes, until it feels as if his head might explode.

The centurion gives the signal and two soldiers lift the wood above their heads, suspending the Christ in midair. The other two soldiers place forked poles under the beam, carrying it toward the empty stipe. The weight of Christ's body pulls on his wrists. Each inch of movement wrenches him, sometimes swinging his torso forward. Every wound inflicted up till now fades in proportion to this.

On the center stipe a sign hangs, identifying Jesus and his crime. Fitting

the crossbeam into the notch on the stipe, the soldiers push on the poles until it snaps into place. Jesus presses his feet against the wood, trying to lift himself from the suffocating hold of the crossbeam.

Positioning his left foot on top of the right, and pressing them both down, a soldier drives the final nail through Jesus' arches. Once again, little blood is shed, but an intense ache grips the muscles in Jesus' legs. He hangs from a cross between two criminals, only a few feet from the ground. The soldier's job is done and those left to watch settle in for the long wait.

Does Jesus close his eyes, focusing on the treasure he will buy with his broken body? Does the agony in his feet remind him of the enemy whose head he will soon bruise? Does he look around, taking note of those who have come to his crucifixion? Or does he scan the vast city of Jerusalem, weeping once again at their spiritual poverty?

The Son of Man is lifted up and thereby will one day draw all men to himself. But for now the searing spasms in his arms and legs are a tortuous reminder that death is not easy and will not come quickly. There are battles yet to fight, victories not quite won and a price not yet paid for the sins of a dying world.

Respond

Contemplate this moment when Jesus is raised up on a cross to die. Consider all He has been through up to this point in preparation for it. Spend a few minutes thinking about each of the three nails as they go into His flesh. Try to comprehend what He may have experienced as the crossbeam was attached to the stipe.

Beyond the physical agony, consider that few were there to support Him—His closest followers (except John) have not shown their faces since Gethsemane. Also, ponder the shame of a crucifixion—where everyone can see you and the crime for which you are condemned. When you feel you

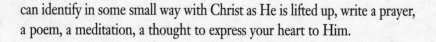

can identify in some small way with Christ as He is lifted up, write a prayer, a poem, a meditation, a thought to express your heart to Him.

A Prayer

Jesus, my Jesus, hanging in the wind, sun burning, body bare save for a loincloth and wounds too many to count. I wonder why you hold onto life amidst Golgotha's death-grip. You said if you were lifted up you'd draw all men to you. Is this what you meant? Lifted up like this? The sheer lunacy of such a plan perplexes me still. Yet you hang there and I am irresistibly drawn to your side. I cannot turn away—not now, not ever.

CHAPTER SIX

CRUCIFIXION

*Knowing that you were not redeemed with perishable things like silver
or gold . . . but with precious blood, as of a lamb, unblemished
and spotless, the blood of Christ.*

1 Peter 1:18–19

Recently I had an interesting discussion with several friends concerning our grasp of Christ's death as children. Some of us remembered Sunday school plays and pictures, others the "Stations of the Cross," and some confessed that "Jesus dying on the cross" offered little more than sentimental significance for them in earlier years. We talked of our own children and wondered whether they were faring better than we had.

One friend shared a unique approach. As a child she dreaded going to the dentist. The thought of having her mouth pulled, pried, filed, and drilled in the dental chair would cause her to tremble with fear. Her mother took advantage of this by encouraging her to focus on the crucifixion.

"Think of Jesus dying for you—a little pain is nothing. Think of Jesus," her mother would say on the way to the dentist.

My friend tells how she envisioned Jesus dying for her. Sitting in the dentist chair she would focus first on the nails in His hands, then the nails in His feet, then the crown of thorns, and so on.

We laughed as we talked, agreeing that her mother's idea was a novel one. Yet she shared how from her earliest years she never doubted God's

great love for her. Even today, anytime she experiences physical pain she automatically thinks of Jesus. Her place in His heart is written deeply on her soul as a result of trained reflection on His dying moments.

Discussions like this force me to evaluate my own life . . . my children . . . my ministry. How am *I* embracing Christ's painful sacrifice on my behalf? What am *I* doing to pass on the reality of God's great love seen in His battered and bloody Son? Where does all this fit in *my personal journey* of faith?

There is a strange dichotomy between the Cross of Christ and the cross of Christian culture. We wear it in beautiful chains around our necks—Christ wore it in bloody stakes through His hands and feet. We display it on bumper stickers and posters with pride, but shame consumed the One who hung there for hours. We hold it close and sense heaven—Christ embraced it and encountered hell.

Our sanctuaries display a cleansed version of the Cross—no blood, no struggle, no filth of sin—solely a monument to resurrection power. We celebrate the passion of Christ once a year, but for most of us the journey from Good Friday to Easter is a short one.

Somehow the horror of Jesus' final days eludes us as we bask in the glow of His ascension.

It's almost as if we've gotten beyond the Cross, though surely that has never been our intention. As believers, we want it to be central to our faith, but struggle to find a practical place for it in our lives.

What would it look like if we did? A morbid fascination with grim details? An aura of morose resignation settling in our souls? Sackcloth . . . ashes . . . melancholy chants from monotone choirs? Surely not.

But if no greater love has ever been seen than when Christ lay his head on the crossbeam at Calvary, we must find a way to be consumed by it. If it took not gold or silver, but precious blood to secure our redemption, we must comprehend the incomprehensible. If God's glory is a jewel hidden in

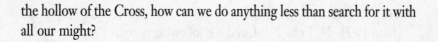

the hollow of the Cross, how can we do anything less than search for it with all our might?

23. FORGIVENESS

What do you weep at, if you do not weep at this?

Dante Alighieri

Reflect

The next several days we will be at the foot of Jesus' cross.[1] Make sure you have enough time and a quiet place to focus. Rest in the compassionate presence of God who loves you and gives His life for you. Softly, slowly speak or sing the words to the following old hymn.

And Can It Be That I Should Gain?
Charles Wesley

And can it be that I should gain
An interest in the Savior's blood?
Died He for me, who caused His pain?
For me, who Him to death pursued?
Amazing Love! How can it be
That Thou, my God, shouldst die for me?

He left His Father's throne above,
So free, so infinite His grace!
Emptied Himself of all but love,
And bled for Adam's helpless race;
Tis mercy all, immense and free;
For O my God, it found out me.
Amazing love! How can it be
That Thou, my God, shouldst die for me?

117

Read

John 19:23–24; Luke 23:34; and the following narrative.

> *But Jesus was saying, "Father, forgive them; for they do not know what they are doing."*
>
> Luke 23:34

At the crossroads of Jerusalem, the hustle and bustle of life goes on. Travelers stop now and then as they pass the hill where three criminals are being executed today. It's a disturbing sight, though, and most hurry to their business within the city.

Those who've walked up the hill to watch the crucifixions form an eclectic group—religious leaders with heads held in haughty disdain, soldiers there to do a job, and curious onlookers who hope for some entertainment from this one said to be possessed with magical powers.

There is another group, separate from the rest. Several women and one man huddle as far as possible from the cross, weeping and holding each others hands. Many recognize John as one of Jesus' followers, his arm around an older woman whose red eyes glance occasionally at the center cross.

Fever flushes through Jesus as he searches the faces in the crowd. Feeling suffocated, he raises himself up on his feet, the only way to exhale and relieve the constriction in his chest. But jolts of pain shoot through his calves and, after only a moment, he must drop down again.

The soldiers, callous from exposure to a thousand days like this one, look for ways to occupy the time. Loud laughter bursts from their midst as they entertain each other with crass stories and off-color jokes. Those in charge of the crucifixion flank the three crosses. They must stay to the end, making

sure no one takes a body down before proof of death.

One of them notices the pile of clothing on the ground at Jesus' feet. Calling to the others, he asks how they should divide it. They examine each piece, shaking their heads. Not much worth having this time. Everything is saturated with dried blood except the head covering. Someone must have removed it before the scourging.

The captain quickly claims it for himself, while the others haggle over the rest. One takes the torn sandals, another the girdle, and a third the robe. The only thing left is the inner tunic. It is so stained one cannot see the original color. Someone suggests they tear it into four parts—the only fair way to dispose of the fifth piece of clothing, worthless though it might be.

As they look for a good place to rip it, they cannot find any seams. Turning it over and over, they are amazed. Superstitious and fearful of the strange garment, no one wants to tear it. Laughing and passing the crusty cloth around, they decide on a guessing game with their fingers. Soon one wins, placing the seamless tunic with his things.

Above them the three condemned to die are silent, save an occasional groan or cry from one of the robbers. Jesus does not make a sound. The soldiers look them over and, satisfied that death is not imminent, take their positions once again.

Father, forgive them; for they do not know what they are doing.

Those near the cross are startled by the voice of the criminal in the center. What a strange thing to say. Some draw closer as if to hear him a little better. It is difficult to read the expression on his face after having uttered his first words from the cross. Both gentleness and anguish cloud his eyes.

Who tugs at his heartstrings this moment? Cold and calculating soldiers who have no idea that he may one day save their souls? Stony-hearted priests and elders who've made an idol of their rules and abandoned the living God? Passersby whose lives are so empty they find diversion in the horror of a crucifixion?

Seven times Jesus will find the fortitude to lift himself and speak cryptic words as he hangs from the cross. But in this first moment, his heart bleeds for an eternity of souls damned to live under Satan's dominion. And opening his mouth, the compassion that has compelled him to walk each step thus far, streams from his soul.

Father, forgive them; for they do not know what they are doing. In the unseen realm, God the Father gently nods his head, and angels' hearts break at such amazing love.

Respond

Close your eyes and come to this moment at the Cross. Watch the soldiers laugh and joke as they divide Jesus' clothes. Smell the sweat in the air as the morning sun burns down. Hear the rumble of conversation among the high priests. Now look at Jesus hanging there. See His eyes on you. Hear Him speak tender words of forgiveness for every act of sin, rebellion, apathy, or disobedience you have ever committed or will commit.

Read Romans 5:8, very slowly. Worship God and thank Him. Write a prayer based on this truth in your journal.

A Prayer

Dearest Savior, I hear your voice breaking through the heat of a summer morning and the busyness of my days. . . . And I am back there— standing at your feet with heartless soldiers and hardhearted priests. I too have sealed your fate with my sins and am in desperate need of compassion. So tenderly you offer forgiveness to them . . . to the world . . . to me. Your voice descends like a gentle rain on the desert of my heart until I am soft and pliable in your nail-scarred hands.

24. KING OF THE JEWS

*Behold what great contempt hath the Lord of Majesty endured, that his
confusion may be our glory; his punishment our heavenly bliss! Without
ceasing impress this spectacle, O Christian, on thy soul!*

Dionysius

Reflect

Come to God's throne today in reverence and awe for the power He
holds over all things. Affirm His right to be Lord over your own life. Humble yourself before Him, asking Him to purify you from sin. Thank Him
for the price He paid that you can come boldly into His throne room.

Read Psalm 29 aloud as a praise to the King of kings. Write a prayer of
worship and exaltation, personalizing His status in your own life.

Read

John 19:19–22 and the following narrative.

And above His head they put up the charge against Him which read,
"THIS IS JESUS THE KING OF THE JEWS."

Matthew 27:37

For a moment, stillness settles in the air at Golgotha. Indifferent soldiers
close their eyes for a morning nap. Others converse quietly, wondering how
long they will have to wait for the condemned to take their final breaths.
The group of women with John continue to hold each other helplessly in
the distance, fresh tears flowing each time they look up.

The number of priests and elders has dwindled. Those still here seem anxious. Whispering among themselves, they look back toward Jerusalem as if waiting for someone or something.

Jesus presses his feet together, digging his toes into the wood to lift himself up again. He spews out air, then gasps like a drowning swimmer who knows he is about to go under. His battered face has taken on a purplish hue, making him look grotesque and surreal. It is almost impossible to recognize him.

He drops back down, his face contorting with pain as the weight of his body hangs from his weak arms. The inscription that his head covered a moment ago, is now smeared with blood. Yet the words written on it are visible even to those on their way to Jerusalem. *This is Jesus the King of the Jews.*

The import and symbolism of such a title is not lost on Caiaphas, the chief priest. Even now, his representatives have gone to demand Pilate change the words. The very thing that riled him about this rabble-rouser is now proclaimed in three languages for the whole world to see. How dare Pilate give Jesus of Nazareth such a designation?

This is Jesus the King of the Jews. These are sacred words, written in the language of the Hebrew Torah. They are powerful words, written in the language of the Roman conqueror Caesar. And they are universal words, written in Greek, the language that will soon record the Gospel of Christ for all the world and every generation to come.

The stillness is broken by the return of the three priests. Their visit to Pilate has not been successful. Quickly they relate their story to the others. They hoped for a title identifying Christ's real crime—treason.

When Pilate refused, they pleaded with him to at least add the words "He said I am" to the title, so everyone would know this was a false claim by a crazy zealot. But Pilate was adamant.

"What I have written, I have written" was his final response.

Caiaphas is furious. He questions the others, his voice getting louder and angrier. His hatred for the Roman procurator takes on new depth.

The soldiers on guard duty, aroused by the noisy priests, begin to pace from cross to cross. If only this would go a little quicker. The one in the middle surely can't last too long, but the other two could stay alive well beyond daylight.

One of the soldiers overhears what the priests are saying and for the first time examines the words written above each criminal. What a peculiar inscription above the beaten one.

This is Jesus the King of the Jews.

How easy it would be for Jesus to live up to his unbidden title even now. For an instant, does he long to strike lightning on the pompous priests or rattle the ground beneath the indifferent soldiers? Does he want to demonstrate his royal heritage, to display his majestic might? Can the King of kings recall the comfort of his awesome throne at all, as he hangs from a cross on a hill called Golgotha?

For now the King wears a crown of thorns. The royal robes hang on the doorpost of heaven's gates, for bloody stripes and gaping wounds now adorn the shoulders of their owner. And the weight of a sin-sick world hangs from the nail-pierced hands that once fashioned it into being. Jesus is dying, but how slow the death.

Respond

Consider the physical agony Jesus now faces as He must lift himself up on His feet in order to exhale. See the suffering on His face as He does so. Know that to even look at Him is sickening. *So His appearance was marred more than any man and His form more than the sons of men* (Isaiah 52:14).

Yet He is still the King of kings and Lord of lords. Contemplate the love that keeps Him from even now asserting His rightful place. Kneel at His feet and worship Him.

A Prayer

My King, I am your subject even now as your face, marred beyond recognition, looks down at me. I can still see the compassion in your weary eyes. I feel the weight of my sin pressing your shoulders down each time you must drop, your arms the only support your body knows. And I bow down. I wash your feet with my tears, dear and precious Redeemer. What more can I do to ease your pain?

25. MOCKED

And age by age the Lord Christ is crucified. And we too have crowded eagerly to Calvary and nailed Him to His cross, and laughed up into His face, and watched Him die, and gone our way well pleased and much relieved that we have hustled Him out of the way—yes, even we.

Arthur John Gossip

Reflect

Spend a few minutes becoming still and serene in God's presence today. Breathe deeply of His love and commitment to you. Breathe out distractions, concerns, and fears. Enjoy the reality of His very personal love for you.

Rest in the knowledge that everything He suffered, He suffered on your behalf; every sin He bore, He bore for you; every insult He endured, He endured for your sake. Offer Him a heart of gratitude.

Read

Mark 15:29–30 and the following narrative.

*And those who were passing by were hurling abuse at Him, wagging
their heads and saying, ". . . If You are the Son of God,
come down from the cross."*

Matthew 27:39–40

Another day, another crucifixion on the mount outside Jerusalem. Within the city, pilgrims prepare food for the Sabbath. The smell of unleavened bread wafts through the air as children play in the streets. From home to home, the conversation touches on the carpenter of Nazareth convicted of treason. Some brag of having seen him do miracles. Others scoff at such nonsense.

The sun beats heavily down on those condemned to die. Jesus sweats profusely, his body rapidly dehydrating. Overcome by chills, he shakes from head to toe. Throbbing wrists pound the pulse of his heart like a drum inside his head.

Feeling faint, he lifts himself to exhale. This time his calves knot up immediately. He falls, wrenching his arms, dislocating one of his shoulders. Tortured with pain, his eyes fly open and he almost passes out.

A loud voice disrupts the rumble of conversation around the crosses. "Aha! There he is. Just look at him."

Some who've wandered by from Jerusalem watch Jesus, shaking their heads in contempt. "Hey—you up there! You—you who said you could destroy the temple and build it in three days! Save yourself, then!"

Laughter breaks out among them. Surely this isn't the man who roared through the temple just yesterday! Where is his pious power now? Repulsive to look at and a disappointment to those hoping for some messianic magic, Christ hangs in silence before the taunting crowd.

If You are the Son of God, come down from the cross!

What does the suffering servant feel as they flaunt his impotence in his face? Is the physical agony so great he is oblivious to their jeers? Or does he hear their laughter and long for a touch of kindness from someone, somewhere? What must it be like to know those who ridicule him will face an eternity in hell if he does as they demand?

If You are the Son of God, come down from the cross!

Others watch in dismay. Why won't Jesus do something? Is he really going to die? Was every miracle a sham, every word of wisdom a pretense? Flickering flames of hope are slowly extinguished in those who thought it would be different. The would-be messiah will not come down.

Some turn to leave. There will be no miracles, and the gruesome moment of death on a Roman cross is not worth waiting for. Others continue to sneer, jabbing at Jesus like jesters of the macabre. And the only one who could change things now, fights for every agonizing breath. The Son of Man still has much to suffer.

Respond

The physical torture of Jesus is immense, but we now move to psychological torture. Consider the kind of atmosphere surrounding the cross as Jesus suffers so. Hear the loud, jeering voices challenging Him to prove himself. Imagine the intensity of emotions the people feel—contempt, disgust, disappointment, hopelessness, anger, insecurity, or others. See their words like arrows piercing the heart of the One who dies even now for them. Imagine you are one of them—ridiculing Him, rejecting Him, dismissing His claims to Deity.

Confess to Him the times you have taken His suffering lightly, have held it at a distance, never seeing yourself in the abuse He suffered. He suffered for your sake and for the world.

Read Hebrews 2:10. Meditate on the words "it was fitting" as you con-

template all Jesus has endured on Calvary so far. Offer Him your love, adoration, and worship. Write a prayer of thanksgiving based on this verse.

A Prayer

O Lord, how little they understood why you hung there on Calvary. They created you in their own image, and when you didn't perform, they were angry. They just didn't know, did they? So many times I have demanded you do as I ask, dismissing your claim on my life when you didn't. I stand here with the mockers, passersby who missed completely the eternal significance of your impending death. And in my selfishness I too miss it day after day. Forgive me, dying Savior, for actions that speak louder than words.

26. SCORNED

Around the Silent Sufferer surged the brutal slaughter and flung its showers of barbed sarcasm in His holy face. The Prisoner has become the sport of the executioners.

William Henry Bierderwolf

Reflect

Allow a sense of peace to fill your heart as you come to the Cross today. Ask God to speak to you, to open your heart to His great love and compassion for you personally. Ask Him for the privilege of sharing in His suffering.

Psalm 22 is a prophecy of Jesus' time on the cross. It tells us more of what He thought as He hung there. Slowly read Psalm 22:1–13, seeking to understand what He felt as you prepare to contemplate the Cross.

Read

Matthew 27:41–43 and the following narrative.

In the same way the chief priests also, along with the scribes, were mocking Him among themselves and saying, "He saved others; He cannot save Himself."

Mark 15:31

As if on cue, the priests and elders take up the ridicule of Christ that the passersby began. With hostility in their hearts, they banter among themselves loud enough for Jesus to hear as he hangs above them.

He saved others; he cannot save himself.

"Yes. If he is God's chosen one—the Christ, then let's see him save himself!"

Jesus watches but says nothing. Is he envisioning what would happen if he did save himself? Can he see demons binding those below, sealing their slavery to sin for eternity? Or does he reminisce over his own words to his followers, *If you want to save your life, you must lose it.* . . .

Self-righteous glee fills the priests as they gloat over their prisoner's condition. Their taunts become more contemptuous, pride filling their hearts.

"Look—there's the *King* of Israel!"

Raucous laughter peppers the air at the absurd idea. "Sure. He's a *King*, so let him come down from the cross—then we'll believe in him!"

Nodding in sarcastic agreement, the elders glance at the Christ, wondering what he will say or do now.

What can he say? What words could change the evil in the hearts of men who glory in his humiliation? What can he do? Come down from the

cross, commanding the allegiance of all mankind? How well he understands that if he did, the price for sin would remain on their heads, a price none of them could hope to pay.

Throughout the ridicule, Caiaphas has stood aloof, arms folded, enjoying this moment of triumph. The envy that once ate at his insides has turned to loathing. He remembers the claims Jesus made only a few hours ago. What a stupid fool.

"He trusts in God. If God loves him so much, let him deliver him right now. After all, he says he is God's own Son!"

Once the chief priest speaks, most of the crowd joins in the revelry on Calvary. Soldiers, inebriated from the wine they have drunk all morning, revert to their earlier game of pretending Jesus is a king.

A couple make grandiose bows before the cross. Another holds up a chalice with the sweet beverage and says, "Come now, O King of the Jews. It is time for you to save yourself!"

Snickering, they stagger around the cross, toasting each other in gaiety at the game that provides a break from the monotony of the day.

Like a roar the scorn at Golgotha reaches the portals of heaven. Myriads of angels mourn, every one of them yearning to jerk the stakes from Jesus' hands and feet. Love for lost humanity still binds the Father and Son together. The Savior of the world will not save himself and let mankind be damned to the hopelessness of hell.

Respond

Many people minimize the price Christ paid for our sins because they believe since He was God, He had the power to do whatever He wanted to as He hung there, or because He knew He would rise again. This is exactly why the price He paid was so great. He could have drawn on His supernatural strength at any moment. He could have forced the issue of His deity,

but He chose not to. He chose to embrace the Cross as a man, impotent and unable to change things.

This is true love. Consider how He endured the pain, the scorn, the agony of it all, when He had the force of the universe at His disposal. Contemplate what this kind of love means to you. Respond in adoration and worship. Write some words expressing your own sense of indebtedness to Christ.

A Prayer

I wish they understood, my Savior, why you wouldn't save yourself. That you loved them too much to leave them in darkness. That you love me too much to destroy my only hope of freedom. That you love us too much to let us wander forever like sheep without a shepherd. I don't want to mock you, my Lord, by embracing your deity and ignoring your suffering as a man. I will not run to the Resurrection without lingering here, where men scoff and you hang in agony and do not save yourself.

27. TWO RESPONSES

When the true meaning of the Crucifixion dawns upon us, then the whole sordid, bloody, painful death shall make us tremble before its glory.

Ben M. Herbster

Reflect

Make a conscious effort to stop the activity in your mind as you come before the Lord this moment. Slow your thoughts down until you can focus on Him. Consider the holy calling He has given you to participate in His sufferings. Ask Him to make this understandable to your heart through His Holy Spirit. Read the following words of Thomas à Kempis, reflecting on them and on your own life.

Jesus hath now many lovers of His heavenly kingdom, but few bearers of His Cross. Many He hath that are desirous of consolation, but few of tribulation. Many He findeth that share His table, but few His fasting. All desire to rejoice with Him, few are willing to endure any thing for Him. Many follow Jesus unto the breaking of bread; but few to the drinking of the cup of His Passion. Many reverence His miracles, few follow the shame of His Cross (*The Imitation of Christ*).

Pray for divine revelation into the condition of your own heart as you contemplate the Cross today.

Read

Luke 23:39–43 and the following narrative.

And He said to him, "Truly I say to you, today you shall be with Me in Paradise."

Luke 23:43

The chorus of mockery surrounding Jesus swells with dissonant notes. Drunken soldiers, pious priests, and sordid onlookers take turns deriding the one who says nothing in return. So intent are they in their scornful quest, none notice the sky swallowing the sun at midday.

One of the thieves joins the jeers and taunts. Death by crucifixion clutches his throat and fear tears at his mind. Hope is slipping away. Finally, hoisting himself up on his feet in rage, he rails at the one crucified beside him.

"Well, are you the Christ or not? Why don't you save yourself and us

then?" Energy spent, he sags back down, rolling his eyes in disgust.

Jesus looks at him sadly. The thief turns his face away, escaping into his lonely torment.

"How can you say such words?" A weak voice laments from the other side of Jesus.

"Don't you fear even God himself? You are here, condemned to die. You and I—we deserve to be here for the crimes we committed. But this man has done nothing wrong."

Forcing his words into the muggy air before his knees collapse, the repentant thief stares past Jesus to his comrade in crime. His words fall on deaf ears. For a moment, the sounds of scorn fade into the distance.

"Jesus."

Through his hazy distress Jesus slowly turns his head to his right. No one has ever addressed him with such familiarity.

"Jesus, will you remember me when you come into your kingdom?"

What an ironic plea offered to the one whose royal reign must seem a fantasy in this place. What does Jesus feel as the poignant words break through his silent reverie? Surrounded by scoffers, what might it mean to hear this solitary voice of support?

Jesus opens his mouth, but cannot speak. Summoning every bit of energy left in his body, he lifts himself, and between gasps for air, calls, "Truly, I . . . say to you, today . . . you . . . shall . . . be with me . . . in . . . Paradise."

With me—never have such beautiful words been spoken. Long ago God's heart broke as He ushered His beloved children out of Paradise into a fallen world. In his second word from the cross, Jesus cracks open the door to the garden of God's presence and lets one sinner in. Soon the price will be paid and he will fling the gates wide open to all who accept his sacrifice for their sins. *With me. . . .*

Does the thought of such fellowship invigorate Jesus' heart? Can he glimpse for a moment the joy of eternity with those he suffers for even now?

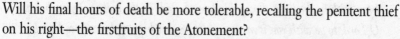

Will his final hours of death be more tolerable, recalling the penitent thief on his right—the firstfruits of the Atonement?

The sky grows gray at Golgotha. Some start down the slope toward home, fearing bad weather. Not even witnessing death by crucifixion is worth tolerating a Jerusalem thunderstorm. The soldier's games have lost their flavor and they settle down in various stages of drunkenness to await the end. Only the priests remain the same—proud, haughty, and consumed with contempt for the one who hangs near death.

And angels rejoice at a sinner saved, though their dance is bittersweet.

Respond

Two men hung on crosses on either side of Jesus. Both had equal access to Him. But consider the differences:

One spoke ridicule; the other spoke truth.

One took no responsibility for his sin; the other saw his need.

One saw Jesus as a ticket to freedom; the other saw Jesus as a Savior.

One hurled abuse; the other pleaded for grace.

One faces eternity in hell; the other entered God's presence that day.

Place yourself there and ask God to show you your own heart. Which thief are you most like? Are there times you can relate to both of them?

Hear Jesus saying these words: *With me . . .* What does it mean to be in God's presence—to be with Him? Spend some time contemplating this—with Jesus on the cross, with Jesus in death, with Jesus in resurrection, with Jesus in victory.

Write a prayer of response.

A Prayer

Dearest dying Savior, deep peace fills my heart when I think of the words you spoke so simply, so eloquently. For this you suffer—that I might be with you. I am overcome by the thought. I live in the warmth of your embrace.

133

I languish in the light of your kindness. I abide in the hollow of your heart. O Lord, to be with you is my one great joy, my hope and reason to live. Let me never settle for less than the simplicity of this.

28. ONE LAST ACT OF CARING

Whenever anything disagreeable or displeasing happens to you remember Christ crucified and be silent.

John of the Cross

Reflect

Prepare your heart to receive from God today and to give back to Him. Spend a few minutes reflecting on how He has blessed your life. Thank Him aloud, specifically for these things. Read Psalm 108:1–5 as a prayer back to God.

Consider for a moment the mother of Christ. Recall how, when a teenager, an angel came and told her she would give birth to the Savior of the world. After her questions were answered, she responded, "Behold, the bondslave of the Lord; may it be done to me according to your word" (Luke 1:38). Think of what her life was like as Jesus' mother. Today, walk with her to the Cross and see her son being crucified.

Read

John 19:25–27 and the following narrative.

Woman, behold, your son!

John 19:26

The Jerusalem sky grows darker with each moment, yet there are no clouds to be seen. Those who remain at Golgotha feel the weight of the air on their skin. A sense of dread settles on the crucifixion crowd. The mockers of a moment ago now wish for a speedy end to the day's events.

Jesus, with eyes shut, pants in short, sharp breaths. After a few minutes his lungs feel like they are exploding within his chest. The simplest thing would be to give in, to let himself be strangled by the air he can't exhale. But it is not yet time.

He pushes down on his feet. Trying to hold himself up with weakened arms, he spews out all the air in his lungs, then gasps for more. There is no relief now to the cramping in his legs. While he can, he looks out over those who still watch. Across the way, he notices a small group walking toward him.

His eyes fill with tears and immense grief covers his face as he recognizes his mother, held by his dear disciple and friend, John. And there are others; two of his aunts, and Mary of Magdala whose devotion to him has been such pure joy in these last months.

What does he feel when his eyes meet those of the woman who bore him in her own body? Does his heart break at the sorrow he inflicts on her? Does he consider how he's tried to prepare her for this? How as a child in the temple, he told her he had to be about his Father's business? Or the day he gently rebuked her, telling her his family were those who chose to follow him and not those related by blood?

Holding himself up with sheer force of his will, he watches the small

group draw close. His mother weeps quietly as she gazes at her beloved son. It is almost too much to bear.

"Woman, behold . . . your . . . son."

Disturbed by the distress in his voice, Mary holds out a hand in the air, as if longing to caress his face. Wracking sobs shake inside her, but she holds her head high, refusing to turn from her son, though her heart tears in two. John tightens his grip around her shoulder, wishing he could do something, feeling powerless.

"Behold, your mother!" Jesus speaks directly to his brave young disciple. Without warning, his legs collapse and he drops. John and Mary watch, hoping for another word. Jesus tries to smile at them, but pain contorts his face into an absurd grimace. He closes his eyes.

John gently turns the mother of Christ from the cross, intent on following his master's final instructions. What more can he do for this one who loved him so in life? Mary of Magdala and the two aunts join the others who watch from a distance, while John and the mother of Christ start the long walk down Mount Golgotha.

How she must ponder the heaviness in her heart. Her baby entered the world bearing the shame of illegitimacy and now he leaves bearing the shame of crucifixion. "Be it done unto me according to Thy word," Mary once said to the angel who illuminated her life with God's plan for her to bear a Savior for the world. She has never wavered in her commitment, but this time the anguish of letting go must be beyond description.

Darkness descends on Golgotha and demons begin their premature celebration of the Redeemer's defeat. The Son of Man it seems has given up, death's grip closing in on him like a vise. But the battle isn't over yet. And though the Prince of Darkness wields his victory flag in glee, the Lord of the universe has not yet finished the fight.

Respond

Wait quietly upon the Lord as you ponder this scene at Calvary. Consider the intense emotions of Jesus as he says good-bye to his earthly mother. Reflect on her unique pain—both that of a mother seeing her son suffer so, and of God's chosen vessel knowing her task is completed in this way. Thank God for her presence at the cross, and for that of John—the one disciple who stayed, and took no thought for his own life.

Consider Mary's words: "Be it done to me according to Thy word." As you reflect on the Cross of Christ, are you able to offer yourself this willingly? Write a prayer expressing your deepest thoughts in this moment at Calvary.

A Prayer

They call you the Suffering Servant, dear Lord of lords. And as I come to watch you die, I hear your voice calling me to take up my own cross and follow you. I want to suffer with you, to be willing to die with you, but instead find myself clinging to rubbish, as if it could satisfy my soul. Give me the courage to pray as your own mother did, "Be it done to me according to Thy word."

29. DARKNESS

Were you there when they crucified my Lord?
Sometimes it causes me to tremble . . . tremble . . . tremble.

Old Negro Spiritual

Reflect

Offer yourself completely to the Lord, letting your heart rest in His presence. The time spent contemplating the Cross today will be serious and

sobering. The result can and should be deeply troubling as you grasp even more of the price Christ paid for your sins.

Read Galatians 3:13 a couple of times, putting your name in the verse. Consider that Christ became a "curse" for you. Write a prayer expressing your heart to God concerning this truth.

Read

Luke 23:44–45 and the following narrative.

* * *

Now from the sixth hour darkness fell upon all the land
until the ninth hour.

Matthew 27:45

* * *

Only a few hours have passed since the nails were first driven through Jesus' wrists and feet. With each grueling moment it becomes harder to hang on. But he has a cup to drink and the final dregs of sin's poisonous nectar await him.

Jesus tightens the throbbing muscles in his arms in order to raise himself once again. The nails tear at his wrists, making the holes larger. Before he can catch his breath, he falls and must push himself up again. After several tries he manages to extend himself long enough to exhale and replenish his lungs with fresh air.

Then, as if from nowhere, an inky film spreads across the sky, turning it completely black. Panic breaks out at Golgotha as people stumble over each other, bewildered by the strange phenomenon. The soldiers grope their way to the crosses, making sure their criminals still hang there. People huddle in small groups, afraid to move, unable to see even one foot in front of

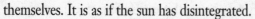

themselves. It is as if the sun has disintegrated.

What is going on in the mind of Christ as light leaves the land? Does he remember the days of Creation when the earth was formless and void and darkness hovered over it? Does the warm memory of a world before sin call him back to the Father's side? Does he long to shout, *Let there be light!* and end this noontime terror?

Hearts pound fearfully in those who remain. The blackness is almost palpable and it seems the sun will never shine again. Though the air is hot and muggy, a chill settles on the soldiers and priests. The absence of light at midday fills them with despair.

With every second, Jesus swallows more of mankind's sin. Every disobedient deed, every lustful stare, every evil longing, every act of hatred, every transgression ever perpetrated and every sin yet to be committed, flows like poison into his very soul—drink after drink, until he reaches the dregs of the cup. And in the drinking, the depravity of sin encompasses Christ.

He who has never known sin *becomes* the epitome of evil. Darkness oozes in and around him and clutches at his soul, its tentacles dragging him down into the swirling waters of Satan's vile dominion.

And the light of the world is extinguished for a few hours on a hill called Calvary. Men who love darkness rather than light demand a sign, and God gives them a sky that matches the blackness of their own hearts. No greater horror has ever existed in the history of the world than this day when *darkness fell upon all the land.*

Respond

Try to imagine the total darkness that descended on Calvary. First contemplate the physical impact of it. Then reflect on the idea that Light is gone and only the darkness of evil remains. Place yourself in the midst of the most vile circumstances you can imagine where sin reigns and no good exists—no kindness, love, joy, compassion, trust, gentleness, or peace.

The atmosphere is terrifying—hatred, bitterness, lust, greed, rage, lying, cheating, murder, rape, gossip, backbiting—these are only a few of the deeds of darkness. This is what reigns on Calvary when Jesus drinks in the sin of the world and becomes a curse for you and for me. Give yourself enough time to feel the complete despair such darkness demands. Envision your own sins—yesterday's, today's, and tomorrow's—in the cup Jesus drank there.

When you think you comprehend even a little of the price Jesus paid for you in those three hours of darkness, read Colossians 1:13–14. Feel the relief of this truth, rejoice in the wonder of it, and worship your Redeemer with a heart of pure and overwhelming gratitude.

A Prayer

O my God, the darkness frightens me even now. My hands shake and I scream for light. I cannot live except you illuminate my sinful soul. How can you drink this cup? It is a mystery I can't comprehend, but this I know— had you stopped short and refused even the last drop, I would eternally dwell in the vast depravity of darkness. O my God, I fall on my knees.

Notes

1. Compiling all four Gospel accounts offers us seven different sayings of Christ while on the cross. No one Gospel includes all of these, so the narratives will incorporate details from each at various times.

CHAPTER SEVEN

DEATH

Thanks be to God for His indescribable gift!
2 Corinthians 9:15

In a cathedral in Issenheim, Germany, hangs an incredible rendition of the crucifixion of Christ. Painted in 1516 by Matthias Gruenwald, it measures nine by twelve feet. It is an unusual work, not only for its grandeur but because Gruenwald ignored the progressive movement to portray a non-suffering Jesus on the cross. The Jesus of this painting is emaciated, haggard, and truly disturbing to view.

Tradition notes that many Germans in the late 1500s suffered from a disease called St. Anthony's sickness (it may have been epilepsy). As treatment for it, the person was taken to Issenheim and placed before Gruenwald's painting for three days. Only after this time was the patient admitted to the hospital, for it was believed that gazing upon Jesus in His torment at Calvary aided the healing process.

Throughout history many believers have found comfort, healing, and spiritual renewal through the scores of artistic renditions of Christ's death. Yet no paint splashed on canvas, no words penned in purest form, and no images carved of clay can begin to touch the reality of what the Cross of Christ brings to those who trust in the One who died there.

This book is not a theological treatise. I believe as evangelicals we often

devote so much of our time to the intellectual understanding of Christ's death that we lack the fury with which His passion should consume us on a personal level. My primary goal has not been to promote the theology of the Cross, but to draw each of us to His wounded side where we can embrace Him completely in His death.

Still, no contemplation of the Cross would be complete without some awareness of its theological implications for our lives. To that end, I point in the next few paragraphs to some of Calvary's most profound truths. To me, every one of them is a mystery I will not completely grasp until I see my Savior face-to-face.

But what joy even a limited understanding brings. Though you may be familiar with these terms, I encourage you to spend some time with each of them, coming back again and again as you learn to live in the shadow of Calvary day by day.

In the Cross, Christ REDEEMED you.

You were a slave in Satan's camp, placed there because of the debt you owed and could not pay. You were a prisoner of war, spiritually dead with no hope of escape, when Jesus came and defeated the one whose rule controlled your life. By conquering death, Jesus redeemed you from the tyranny of sin, paying the price for your freedom with His own life (Galatians 3:13; Colossians 1:13–14).

In the Cross, Christ ATONED for your sin.

You have done a grievous wrong to almighty God through your indifference and rebellion. Atonement must be made—a gift, a ransom given on your behalf—which might turn Him from His anger toward you. No matter how hard you try or how many good works you might accrue, it won't be enough. The only gift good enough is the pure, unblemished lamb of God. At Calvary, Jesus offered himself on your behalf and God received it. He is angry with you no more (Psalm 49:7–8; Mark 10:45).

In the Cross, Jesus RECONCILED you to God.

You were God's enemy, completely separated from Him, your sin having erected an impenetrable wall. Jesus made peace possible by breaking down this barrier with His own blood. He removed the cause of God's quarrel with you, so that you could come together once again (Ephesians 2:13; Romans 5:10).

In the Cross, Jesus JUSTIFIED you.

You are guilty of the vilest sin and now you stand before the judge who has the power to send you to a prison of eternal damnation. But Jesus stands in front of you, and as God looks He sees not your sin but your complete purity and innocence through the blood of His Son. He calls out, *Not guilty!* It is as if you never committed a crime (Titus 3:6–7; Romans 5:9).

It seems we barely scratch the surface when we seek to enumerate the graces of God at Calvary. The list could go on and on, and of course thousands of volumes have been written to declare the praises of Him who died for you and me. As you come to Christ's final moments on Calvary, let your heart rejoice that Christ suffered unto death so that He might bestow upon you all of this and more!

"What then shall we say to these things? If God is for us, who is against us? He who did not spare His own Son, but delivered Him over for us all, how will He not also with Him freely give us all things?" (Romans 8:31–32)

30. FORSAKEN

There is something infinitely more profound than pathos in the death of Jesus; there is a mystery we cannot begin to touch.

Oswald Chambers

Reflect

Breathe deeply as you settle your heart before God. Release the distractions of your day, concentrating on the presence of Christ in and around you

through His Spirit. Do this until you feel ready to contemplate what God has for you today.

Quietly read Amos 8:9–10, a prophecy of the darkness at Golgotha. Imagine the atmosphere God describes. See rejoicing turning to mourning and happy songs turning to loud, mournful laments at the gloom of a world without Light. Ask God to reveal the reality of this so that you may mourn for His only Son as you come to the Cross today.

Read

Mark 15:34 and the following narrative.

And about the ninth hour Jesus cried out with a loud voice, saying,
"ELI, ELI, LAMA SABACHTHANI?" that is,
"MY GOD, MY GOD, WHY HAST THOU FORSAKEN ME?"

Matthew 27:46

The darkness on Golgotha is so thick that no one dares move. The air wreaks hopelessness. Sweeping depression descends on everyone who attends the crucifixion of Jesus of Nazareth. Some shake with terror, others weep in despair. Priests clutch their phylacteries like good luck charms, but relief doesn't come.

Jesus writhes in agony as he drinks the final drops from sin's vile cup. His back is a mass of infection, raw sores oozing. His grotesque face contorts in the blackness at midday. Thankfully no one can see his repugnant form. When finally he swallows the last of the bitter potion, his body explodes in convulsions of wracking pain.

Flinging himself up with inhuman strength, he screams: *"My God, my God, why have You forsaken Me?"*

The priests, startled at first, smirk at his weakness, but their inexplicable depression deepens. The soldiers, sobered from their drunken states, fight their own internal demons. Abject woe wrenches the hearts of the women who hear their beloved Rabbi scream in the distance.

What evokes such a plea from the innermost being of the crucified One? Is hope completely obscured by the darkness of the sin he carries? Is the onslaught of demonic forces threatening his determination to endure till the end?

"My God, my God, why have You forsaken Me?" he calls to God, but there is no answer. What inner turmoil must plague the son at this severing of his triune soul? From Gethsemane till now, God the Father has refused to intervene. What kind of wretchedness wields its way into His son's heart at such rejection? Does sovereign silence sabotage Jesus' struggle to obey for even an instant?

With great force, he is plunged back down, paralyzing the muscles in his arms. Then, for no apparent reason, the sky starts to lighten. Those near the crosses examine the face of the one who screamed in such distress. How can one explain what they see? For though wracked with pain and battered beyond belief, something strange emanates from his eyes. Is it a look of relief?

And God the Father weeps great sobs, shaking the heavens with His grief. How hard it has been to hold back as He watched His son endure such agony. How He has longed to intervene—to subdue the suffering for even a moment. What torment He has known in every drop of sin His son has drunk.

But love for mankind ties His hands and silences His voice. The price is paid—by the Son who dies and the Father who could save him, but declines on behalf of a lost and dying world.

Respond

It is beyond our human comprehension to fathom what happened when Christ took on the sins of the world. Yet as His followers we must try. Place yourself in that state of darkness once again and listen to Jesus cry from the cross: *My God, my God, why have You forsaken Me?* What would it be like to know your only parent will not help you in your time of greatest need?

In reality, God did not turn His back on Jesus, but chose over and over not to intervene that the price of sin might be paid in full. As you hear Jesus cry out, consider both His pain and the Father's. Consider the agony of watching your only child suffer, knowing you must not reach out to help.

Read Hebrews 5:7–9 and rejoice that He is your source of eternal salvation. Spend some time in worship for all that has been done to purchase you from sin's grip. Write a prayer based on these verses.

A Prayer

Father God, how rarely have I thought of your pain in watching your Son die as He did. I dismiss it with theological theories and lofty explanations. But you were there. You did not leave—that perhaps would have been easier. You stayed and you watched and you wept—and you did nothing. For my sake, my Lord, you refused to act. Truly I am unworthy of such love. I rest in my unworthiness and relish your mysterious passion for one such as I.

31. THIRSTY

How do you approach the thirst of Jesus? Only one secret—the closer you come to Jesus, the better you will know His thirst. Jesus thirsts even now, in your heart and in the poor—He knows your weakness, He wants only your love, wants only the chance to love you.

Mother Teresa

Reflect

Come to the oasis of God's refreshing presence as you seek Him today. Spend a few minutes thanking Him for the living water that is always available for you to drink. Consider what it means to be truly thirsty and unable to quench your thirst.

Another prophecy of the Crucifixion is found in Psalm 69. Read verses 1–4, 20–21, and contemplate the emotions of Christ in His final moments on Golgotha. Ask God to reveal the deeper truths revealed in His cry *I thirst*.

Read

John 19:28–29; Matthew 27:47–49; and the following narrative.

After this, Jesus, knowing that all things had already been accomplished, in order that the Scripture might be fulfilled, said, "I am thirsty."

John 19:28

The faint light spreading across Golgotha stirs groups of onlookers who have been frozen in fear. Many hurry home, anxious to leave the sense of hopelessness they feel around them. The four soldiers, superstitious about the receding darkness, shuffle nervously near the crosses. Conversation flows once again, everyone offering their opinion on the black sky and the loud cry from the middle cross.

One of the priests announces, "Clearly, he is calling for Elijah!" Apprehensive laughter ensues as they discuss the absurdity of such a plea.

The physical pain for Jesus drones on, a persistent vibration in every cell of his failing body. Yet the agony on his face is different now. In the eye of suffering's terrible storm, it seems he has found a place of rest. He looks out

over Jerusalem, recalling his days and nights of devotion to the Father's plan. A sense of completion settles his soul. He has done what he came to do.

Death is near. He pants faster, gasping for air. His lungs ache from the stress and his throat burns with each breath. His heart works harder and harder to pump blood throughout his body.

Dehydrated, and no longer able to swallow, he manages to push himself up enough to call, *I am thirsty*.

What goes through his mind as he speaks? Is it physical thirst that compels him to cry out? Or do the words tell a deeper story? Does he thirst on behalf of a lost and dying world that is desperate for a taste of the living water only he can give? Is he gently reminding those who will follow him that in quenching the thirst of humanity they quench his own thirst—that a cup of water given to the least of these is a cup of water for him?

One of the soldiers grabs a reed from a hyssop plant, putting a sponge on its tip. He dips it in his own cup of cheap wine and holds it to Jesus' lips. The priests and elders, disgusted at the act of kindness, call out barbs and taunts once again.

"Ha! Leave him alone and see if Elijah will come and take him down!"

"Yes. Let us see if Elijah will come and save him now!"

The laughter resumes, though it lacks the force of their earlier sarcasm. The vinegar wine burns Jesus' cracked lips and parched tongue, dripping down his face. The afternoon sun beats on his matted head, and his body shivers uncontrollably.

Within the gates of the city, the celebration of Passover comes slowly to an end. Families have broken bread and offered their finest lambs in sacrifice and thanksgiving to Jehovah. Outside the gates, the Lamb of God steps toward the very threshold of death, becoming the ultimate sacrifice for a world bound by sin.

Respond

Let yourself feel a small sense of the peace that Christ is experiencing on a spiritual level at nearing completion of the work on the Cross. Yet know that the physical pain continues. Imagine His thirst, having had nothing to eat or drink for hours, hanging in the hot sun, tongue swollen and lips cracked and dry. Then consider His longing to give living water to all who want to drink—the longing that allowed Him to endure the nails being driven into His hands and feet. Hear Him say, *I thirst*. Contemplate His voice and these two words for a while. What do they mean to you?

Read Psalm 22:14–18, reflecting on Jesus' state of mind. How will you respond to His thirst? What difference will it make in your own life? Write a prayer of response to Him as He calls to you personally: *I thirst*.

A Prayer

O Jesus, how I long to quench your thirst. I see you there, and I want to offer you a cool glass of water from a fresh spring. For this is what you did for me when my soul dwelt in a dry and thirsty land. You gave to me from the river of life, and now springs flow from me as you promised. I hear you say you thirst and I see the pain in those poor and wretched souls who know no relief, just as you knew none when you died for them. I will quench your thirst, dearest Savior. To a lost and dying world, I will give a cup of water in your name.

32. IT IS FINISHED

*Blessed Redeemer, precious Redeemer, seems now I see Him
on Calvary's tree.*

Avis B. Christiansen

Reflect

Spend some time being silent as you begin today, stilling all the sounds within and without. Breathe in His great love and breathe out your own self-centeredness. Breathe in His commitment to you and breathe out your own petty commitments to things with no eternal value. Ask God to purify your heart.

Read 1 John 3:16. What does this verse say you learn from focusing on Christ's death? Has this become true for you? Do you grasp His deep, passionate love for you personally as you consider His horrible death? Ask God to write this on your heart more fervently, as you hear Jesus' final words to mankind from the cross.

Read

John 19:30 and the following narrative.

When Jesus therefore had received the sour wine, He said,
"It is finished!"

John 19:30

Every eye in the small crowd left at the cross is on Jesus. Death is imminent and many are curious to see how he will go. Passersby who have stayed till the end hope to get their money's worth. Perhaps the would-be king will perform some final miracle. The priests, anxious for him to breathe his final breath, keep a detached vigil at his feet.

The soldier who gave Jesus the wine sees that it has strengthened him some. His eyes, though masked with pain, reflect an inner calm. Unlike most victims of crucifixion, he does not fight the throes of death. Hanging there so still, it appears he has passed on.

But then he moves again. Gingerly he presses his bloody feet into the stipe once again. Lifting only a couple of inches, his eyes scan the vast horizon, then settle on those below. He forces the air from his lungs, then sucks in as much as he can. As if to let everyone know his time has come, he speaks haltingly: "It . . . is . . . finished!"

What images flash across his memory as he utters these final words to mankind? Does his short span on earth now spin like a panorama of events through his mind? Visions of Peter throwing out his nets for the catch of a lifetime, then leaving it all behind to follow him? Parents bringing their children to sit on his lap and be blessed? Adulterers, prostitutes, liars, and thieves coming to him for restoration? Religious leaders hungry for spiritual truth seeking him out in the middle of the night? The blind seeing, the lame walking, the demonized set free, and even the dead coming back to life?

Does he recall the dozens of prophecies concerning him, rejoicing that they are finally fulfilled? Can he hear his Father proclaiming once again, "This is my beloved Son, in whom I am well pleased"?

It is finished. He speaks words replete with symbolism, and some standing there wonder what he means. He could be saying so many things: It is accomplished . . . the debt is discharged . . . the plan has been executed . . . the task is complete. Even the soldiers stop and stare, turning the three words over in their minds.

Satan hears the utterance and gloats in tawdry triumph. He calls for a party, believing he has won after all. Demons dance and toast one another, drunk on their depravity. The Son of God will die like everyone else.

It is finished. Jesus wraps his dying words in an eternity of truth. Through one man sin entered the world, bringing a sentence of death to all mankind. But now the price for that sin is paid in full and the new covenant in Christ's blood takes effect this very moment. Through this one man, eternal life is offered to all who will believe.

It is finished. In his final seconds, as Jesus considers the world for which

he came, perhaps one thought prevails. Finally, the family of man will see what love is and how passionately the Father cares for His creatures. It has cost Him dearly, and many will never understand how much. But from the foundation of the world God's unconditional love has led to this moment when His Son, dying a despicable death on a cross, proclaims, *It is finished.*

Respond

Stop for a moment, breathing in the sense of calm that filled Christ as He saw His completed work. Consider all the days and nights that led up to this—especially the last several hours. Contemplate the suffering that He endured. Hear Him saying to you, naming you by name: *It is finished. Your sins are forgiven. Your debt is paid. You are free. I have redeemed you not with silver or gold, but with my precious blood. You are bought with this painful price. This alone is the joy that compelled me to persevere. You are my joy. It is finished.*

Read Romans 8:31–32. Think of these words in light of your understanding of Christ's death on the Cross. What new meaning do they have? Offer a prayer of worship and thanksgiving based on these verses. Write it in your prayer journal.

A Prayer

O my Father, you are truly for me . . . for me. What in the world can I say to such a thought? You spared nothing for me—not even your own precious Son. For every one of us stained with the sordidness of sin, you delivered Jesus to horrible suffering on Calvary. How can I ever doubt your love? How can I ever question your plans for me? How can I ever distrust anything that comes from you who freely gives me all things?

33. THE END

As you gaze upon the cross, and long for conformity to him, be not weary or fearful because you cannot express in words what you seek. Ask him to plant the cross in your heart. Believe in him, the crucified and now living one, to dwell within you, and breathe his own mind there.

Andrew Murray

Reflect

There are mysteries we will never fully understand concerning the death of Jesus on the Cross. Ask God today to open your spiritual eyes to something new concerning His sacrifice for you. Place your heart at the foot of His Cross, content to spend time meditating, reflecting, and rejoicing at what has happened. Remember Jesus' words to Pilate that the power to take His life comes only from God (John 19:11). Thank Him for making the choice even to the very end that enables your own redemption.

Read

Luke 23:46; Matthew 27:50; and the following narrative.

And Jesus, crying out with a loud voice, said,
"Father, INTO THY HANDS I COMMIT MY SPIRIT."

Luke 23:46

Six hours have passed since the Crucifixion began. The soldiers, sensitive to every nuance of death on a cross, know the end is nigh for the peculiar criminal in the middle. He is going quickly compared to most, but to those

who love him every minute must seem an endless marathon of misery.

At this point he is abhorrent to look at. His hair clings to his head with spit and sweat and blood. His face is ghastly, swollen, bruised, and mangled, the crown of thorns stuck in dried rivulets of blood.

His back resembles raw meat. Lacerated from the scourging, the wounds have bred ugly abscesses in the hours he has repeatedly rubbed against the stipe. The holes in his hands and feet have torn, and his whole body shakes in the tremors of one succumbing to infection.

Watching him now, it is as if time is suspended on Calvary. Almost in slow motion, he lifts himself. Then, with a force that shocks even the most disinterested bystanders, he screams: *"Father, into Thy hands I commit My Spirit."*

With this, he breathes out all the air left in him. His body collapses, and in a final act of humility, Jesus the Christ bows his head, giving up his spirit. He is gone, completing the cycle for which all of creation has longed since Adam first sinned in the Garden of Eden. From the Father he came into the world and now to the Father he returns.

His last words are a mystery to all. This is no sound of defeat, certainly not words of despair. It is the cry of a conqueror and a voice of victory. No one knows quite what to make of it.

All of antiquity has led up to this and all history will point back to it. To many it will seem a foolish thing that one claiming to be God's Son should die like this. But to those who will come to the fountain filled with blood on Golgotha's hill, the war cry Jesus bellows as he embraces death—*Father, into Thy hands I commit My spirit*—is the very power of salvation.

Respond

Can you imagine what it must have felt like to hear Jesus shout these final words? Consider the strength He felt, the complete sense of control He had over His own destiny. Even at the conclusion of such terrible suf-

fering—even while His body shrieks with pain, He cries out with strength and power. Consider the joy He must have felt as He offered His spirit back to the Father from whence He came. What an incredible reunion they must have had. Rejoice with the living God at this moment of victory.

Read Colossians 2:13–14 quietly. Then read it again aloud, placing your name in the passage, turning it into a prayer of praise (e.g., *O God, when I was dead in my vile sin, you made me alive together with you . . .*). Write it out in your prayer journal and commit to rejoicing throughout this day at the truth of it.

A Prayer

O God, I hear your victory cry and I want to shout too. My heart has wept with you and now I rejoice in your joy at going to your Father. I see you leaving that cross, and there stained with your life's blood are my own sins—a certificate of debt I could never pay—nailed to the wood with the nails that once held you there. But you are gone, you have paid it all and I wonder how I can ever express my praise.

34. THE EARTH RESPONDS

But as we gaze, it is not pity that we feel, but a profound reverence, for there on Calvary is the great turning point in the course of human affairs.

Hughell Fosbroke

Reflect

Come to the Lord today with simple gratitude for His great love. Rest in Him for a few minutes, offering words of adoration.

Consider the turning point in history that Jesus' death brought about.

Besides the spiritual impact, think of how our world revolves around the event—our calendar being based on it. Muse for a few minutes on the concept that from this event sprang a religion that has spanned the globe, changing lives in every nation on earth. Ask God to plant a sense of awe within you as you reflect upon the first moments after He died.

Read
Matthew 27:51–53 and the following narrative.

And the veil of the temple was torn in two from top to bottom.

Mark 15:38

The earth reverberates at the death of Jesus of Nazareth on a hill outside Jerusalem. Those around the crosses feel the ground rumbling beneath them. The shaking builds, knocking some off their feet.

Then, without warning, the hillside ruptures, creating crevices large enough to swallow one whole. Rocks disintegrate and confusion runs rampant on Golgotha and throughout the city. The Jews, recalling ancestral stories of God's judgment through acts of nature, wonder if some great sin has taken place.

It is the time of the evening sacrifice, and several priests have made their way to the Temple to burn incense. They, too, feel the ground quaking, and as they clutch tables to keep from falling, something incomprehensible occurs. With a sound like the roar of the sea, the heavy curtain separating them from the Holy of Holies begins to come apart. The fine linen shimmers and shakes, it's shades of purple, violet, and scarlet blending into one.

Frozen, they watch as the veil that normally takes 300 priests to handle

every year on the Day of Atonement, tears in two from top to bottom. It is an awesome and frightening sight to behold. In all its splendor, the Ark of the Covenant with the mercy seat glistens before them. Stunned, the priests back away.

What must they feel as they view that which they've never been allowed to see before? Does the cloud of God's presence hover over the mercy seat as it did in Moses' day? Do they fear the wrath of God who ordained that only one man enter this place once a year? Will some of these priests soon put their faith in Jesus the Messiah as a result of what they've seen here?

The earth continues to convulse, and what happens next defies the wildest imagination. Boulders sealing tombs crack open. Up through the rubble, bodies long dead come to life. No one will ever know how many are given this resurrection gift, but in the coming week many of these dead-brought-back-to-life will shock family and friends as they appear throughout Jerusalem.

One cannot deny that something of supernatural significance is occurring in this place of death. The earth shakes, rocks shatter, and the dead rise. The veil of the temple tears in two, admitting common priests into the Holy of Holies where God's presence resides and the blood of bulls is sprinkled annually to atone for sin. Almighty God acknowledges the death of His Son in a powerful way.

All of these things bear witness to another veil that has been rent—that of Jesus' flesh. His blood is now sprinkled across the altar of history. This sacrificial Lamb atones for sins not once a year but once and for all, leading the way for mankind to live forever in the shadow of God's holy presence.

Respond

Ponder for a moment the freedom you have to enjoy God's presence day in and day out, knowing His Spirit will never leave you. Leviticus details God's plan for a Day of Atonement for the Israelites. Read chapter 16. There we learn that only one person was allowed in the place where God's presence

resided—and then only once a year—to offer sacrifices for the sins of all. If anyone disobeyed they would die.

Now read Hebrews 10:11–22. Thank Jesus Christ for everything about your relationship with Him and salvation through Him. Write a list and offer it up as a sacrifice of praise to the Author of your own salvation.

A Prayer

Jesus, through suffering you lead the way, tearing the wall of separation between God and me in two. I cannot stand back—there is nothing to fear and nothing I must do to become worthy. Through your broken body and spilt blood, I run with joy into the throne room of God's presence. How great my awe in this moment, O perfect High Priest.

35. REACTIONS

And, as you sit and gaze, it will be born in you that only a crucified Savior could meet your need.

William Sangster

Reflect

Sit quietly in God's presence today, rejoicing that He is faithful to meet you here regardless of what you have done or what you feel. The truth that He never leaves or forsakes you is a foundation you can rest in right now.

Read Psalm 96 aloud, personalizing it as a song of praise to the living God who gave himself for you. Rejoice that you are able to proclaim the tidings of His salvation because of His work on the Cross.

Read

Matthew 27:54–56 and the following narrative.

When the centurion, who was standing right in front of Him, saw the way He breathed His last, he said, "Truly this man was the Son of God!"

Mark 15:39

Pandemonium breaks out among the participants in the drama of Calvary. Though the earth is settling down, hearts still pound in fear. Most of those who remain hurry to get away from the crucifixion scene, unaware that the entire universe has been affected by what has happened here. Priests huddle together, discussing their next move.

The four soldiers on duty cautiously approach the dead criminal. Images from the past six hours assault their senses, filling them with apprehension. The centurion in charge holds out his hands, his eyes glued to the face of Christ. The countenance on the dead man is a peaceful one, his bruises and cuts seeming to have faded.

How different is this death from all the others the soldiers have witnessed. Never have they seen one treated so horribly, yet so in control of his final moments. Clearly the one who hangs here determined his own destiny, even to his dying breath. A stillness surrounds the small circle of soldiers, and in awe the centurion speaks: "Truly this man was the Son of God!"

With these words a Roman soldier declares the divinity of Jesus the Christ, bearing witness to his inherent majesty. It is a historical moment, for in his declaration the centurion becomes the first Gentile to recognize and embrace the truth about Jesus of Nazareth.

Far from the cross stands another group. There is Mary of Magdala, whom Jesus once set free from the torment of seven demons. Her shell-shocked eyes stare silently at the body of Christ. There are Jesus' aunts, and other women who left friends and family in Galilee to follow Jesus and min-

ister to him and the disciples from their own resources. Exhausted, they hold each other in quiet grief, weeping no longer.

Some religious Jews, uncertain and frightened by the turn of events, begin to beat at their breasts, pleading for God to have mercy on their souls.

Others who had known Jesus at one time or another now shake their heads in disbelief. The last of the crowd begins to break up and a subdued procession winds its way down Golgotha's hill back to the business of life.

Some are relieved it is over. Many are numb, confused, and emotionally spent. But in the seconds after the death of Jesus on Calvary's cross, one soldier encounters the Savior. In childlike trust, he speaks words of faith, and like millions of others who will join him for centuries to come, nothing will ever be the same.

Respond

Think of what the centurion experienced when he realized who Jesus was. Contemplate the sense of awe that filled him and the faith he demonstrated when he spoke aloud what he saw.

Do you remember when you first discovered the truth about Jesus Christ? Whether it was as a child through a Sunday school book, as a teenager, or as an adult, take the time to reminisce about those moments. Relive in your heart the wonder and fresh awareness that Jesus died for you. Embrace anew the joy of your salvation.

Write a prayer of gratitude for your personal salvation.

A Prayer

Dearest Savior, you died for me when I was still in my sins. You suffered and bled for me when I lived in such darkness of soul that I could only dream there was hope in this world. I relish the moment I first understood your love for me. I remember my complete sense of awe—the tears I couldn't hold back and the ache in my heart at your compassion. I want to return to this

place over and over and over again, lest I ever forget the joy of my salvation or wander from my first love—you, my blessed Redeemer.

36. WATER AND BLOOD

Stand at the foot of the cross, and count the purple drops by which you have been cleansed; see the thorn-crown; mark His scourged shoulders, still gushing with encrimsoned rills. . . . And if you do not lie prostrate on the ground before that cross, you have never seen it.

Charles Spurgeon

Reflect

As you come before the Lord today, consider what it must have been like to have been a Jew celebrating Passover. For centuries, fathers have passed down to their children the glorious miracle of God sparing them from death when they put the blood of a pure, unblemished lamb over their doorposts in Egypt (see Exodus 12).

Read Ephesians 1:7–8. Reflect on the fact that Jesus' blood is a sign over you, that you may escape terrible judgment and punishment and embrace new life. Jesus is our Passover Lamb. Muse on this for a few moments.

Now, very slowly, read 1 Peter 1:17–19. Read it again, offering specific words of thanksgiving for everything it tells you about yourself, and your relationship to Christ.

Read

John 19:31–37 and the following narrative.

And he who has seen has borne witness, and his witness is true; and he knows that he is telling the truth, so that you also may believe.

John 19:35

As evening draws near, a few priests keep watch over the three crosses. The two thieves continue to groan occasionally and raise up, spewing out air. The blasphemer in the middle appears to be dead, but one can never be too sure. With the Sabbath approaching, Caiaphas worries that they won't be dead before sundown.

Sacred law is clear on this, no criminal is to hang from a tree overnight. With it being Passover week, and tomorrow the Sabbath, the thousands of pilgrims who've come to Jerusalem to worship will certainly question his own authority if these bodies are left to hang.

Disturbed, Caiaphas sends one of the elders with an urgent message to Pilate, requesting he order the soldiers to break the bones of the dying men. Once this is done and they can no longer lift themselves up to exhale, they will suffocate in a matter of minutes. As they wait, the chief priest paces impatiently, wanting to be done with the whole sordid saga.

Finally, a runner approaches, handing the order to the centurion in charge. It is what he expected. As a final act of punishment and to hasten death, his men must break the legs of the three criminals.

Picking up a large iron bar, he motions to one of the soldiers to initiate the task. The soldier nods and moving to the thief on the right, strikes a viscous blow just below the knees. The criminal cries out, then collapses. The bar is handed to another soldier who does the same to the thief on the left.

The third soldier takes the bar and approaches Jesus. As he starts to

swing, the centurion motions to him to wait. Clearly this one is dead, and has been for a while. Why bother breaking his legs? The three soldiers watch with questioning looks. The centurion knows that Pilate will want proof of death, but for some reason feels compelled to keep them from breaking this one's bones.

Reaching down, he pulls out his lance and faces Jesus. Quickly he plunges it into his heart, jumping back to avoid the blood gushing out. But what a strange fluid streams from the side of Christ. At first it seems to be normal thick red blood from the lower heart cavity. But then a clear liquid much like water flows out freely.

The centurion and other soldiers stare curiously. What an odd crucifixion this has been. Nothing about this prisoner's behavior has been typical. Now, he bleeds blood and water, a sight they've never seen in all the hundreds of executions they've witnessed.

The crowd has thinned to a handful on Mount Golgotha. The last of the priests and elders, content that Jesus is dead, hurry home before the sun sets in the west. The soldiers begin to clean up the area around the crosses where debris from the day is scattered.

As news spreads throughout Jerusalem of the mysterious phenomenon of blood and water flowing from the carpenter's side, some pause to consider what it might mean. There are those who say Jesus died of a broken heart. In days to come, his followers will understand his sacrifice in the blood that flowed, and cleansing from sin in the water that followed.

One day, this scene will flash in front of every person who has ever lived. Every eye will gaze at Jesus' pierced side, and they will mourn as if they have lost their only son, for they, too, played a part in his gruesome death. But today on a hill outside Jerusalem, only a few stragglers witness the amazing enigma of blood and water flowing from the side of the lamb that is slain on behalf of mankind.

Respond

Spend some time gazing at Jesus in death on Calvary. Allow your mind to recall various scenes from this place—the words He spoke, the compassion He showed, the gentleness He demonstrated, and the choice He continued to make to offer himself on your behalf till the very end. As you contemplate these things, worship Him.

Read Zechariah 12:10 and Revelation 1:7. Look on the one that you, too, have pierced with your own sin. Feel a sense of mourning at your part in His death, but also rejoice that He will come again in glory as the King of kings and all will understand the price He paid. Offer words of praise for this reality. Write a prayer of thanksgiving.

A Prayer

Jesus, even now, I look at you—at your side as it flows with water and blood. It is a fountain I cannot drink from enough, dearest Savior. I feel your heart break for me and I know that I, too, have pierced you with my indifference, my rebellious clutch at control, and my callous disregard for the price you paid to change all this. I see in your blood the great sacrifice and I take comfort in the living water that ever flows from your side. Wash me here, Lord, and I will be whiter than snow.

37. TAKEN DOWN

For in the Cross of Christ, as in a splendid theater, the incomparable goodness of God is set before the whole world. The glory of God shines, indeed, in all creatures on high and below, but never more brightly than in the Cross.

Calvin's St. John

Reflect

We have walked the entire journey with Christ to the cross and soon His body will be taken down. What joy we can embrace as we comprehend His great love on Calvary. Quiet your heart before God, and read (or sing) slowly the words to the following old hymn. Do this several times, until your heart is set toward your precious Redeemer.

When I Survey the Wondrous Cross
Isaac Watts

When I survey the wondrous cross
On which the prince of glory died,
My richest gain I count but loss,
And pour contempt on all my pride.

Forbid it, Lord, that I should boast,
Save in the death of Christ my God.
All the vain things that charm me most—
I sacrifice them to His blood.

See, from His head, His hands, His feet,
Sorrow and love flow mingled down;
Did e'er such love and sorrow meet,
Or thorns compose so rich a crown?

Were the whole realm of nature mine,
That were a present far too small:
Love so amazing, so divine,
Demands my soul, my life, my all.

Has your time spent at the Cross produced this kind of response?

Read

Mark 15:42–47; John 19:38; and the following narrative.

165

And Joseph took the body and wrapped it in a clean linen cloth.

Matthew 27:59

In Jerusalem, lavish preparations are being made for the evening meal at Castle Antonia. Pilate, exhausted from the long day's events, soberly sips a glass of wine. The Jew from Nazareth continues to plague his thoughts. Visions of death by crucifixion linger and the procurator becomes increasingly agitated.

A persistent pounding at the door startles him from his morbid musing. A servant informs him that Joseph from the town of Arimathea, a member of the Sanhedrin, requests an audience. Now what? Pilate shakes his head. Will this thing ever go away? But Joseph is a wealthy and powerful man. It would not be prudent to refuse to see him. He instructs the servant to bring him in.

Joseph strides forward with brisk confidence. "Sir, it is the very sacred custom of my people to bury the dead before sundown. Time is short and I would like to request permission to take the body of Jesus of Nazareth and prepare it for burial."

Pilate examines the distinguished religious leader. How strange that one of those responsible for Jesus' death would now want to give him an honorable burial. Still, Pilate relishes the thought of being done with the whole thing.

"Is he dead, then?" He asks. "I must find out first. Then I will decide."

Quickly a messenger is sent to question the centurion at Golgotha. He returns, assuring Pilate that Jesus has been dead for some time. With a sense of great relief, Pilate signs the orders to turn the corpse over to Joseph. Finally, he can be rid of this confusing criminal who has turned his life upside down in one day.

Joseph hurries back to Golgotha, apprehension stirring within. What has compelled him to do such a thing? Surely he will lose everything: reputation, status, perhaps even his livelihood. Why take such a risk? Is he simply demonstrating the duty of a pious Jew to make sure the dead are buried before sundown? Does he regret not speaking up on Jesus' behalf just hours ago at the trial? Or is this his first act of faith in the Messiah he has so eagerly watched all his life?

On the way out of town, Joseph stops at a market stall and purchases a large piece of clean, soft linen. As he approaches the incline up Golgotha, he is sickened by what he sees. Flies hover around the body of Christ and crows circle above, ready to devour the decaying flesh. He is shocked at Jesus' physical condition.

Sobered, he hands the orders to the centurion who reads the paper, glancing up at Joseph with relief and respect. He directs the other soldiers to the cross where Christ's emaciated body hangs. One of them grips the nail in Jesus' feet with a large tool, working it back and forth until it comes out. With the Y-shaped poles, they lift the cross-beam off the stipe and lay it on the ground.

Joseph watches, fighting emotions he can't explain, as they remove the nails from Jesus' wrists. Pulling the beam from under the inert body, the centurion turns to him and nods. The honorable religious leader of the Jews kneels beside the form of a man he barely knew and surely never understood, grieved that he has waited so long to come to him.

Laying the cloth out, he gently rolls the body onto it. The simple task distresses him. Scanning the horizon, he sees the soldiers already moving toward town. He must hurry, there is little time before sundown.

Joseph is not alone. Far in the distance, a small group of women watch every move he makes. Though their hearts long to be the ones preparing their Rabbi for burial, they know they cannot approach this esteemed member of the Sanhedrin. They will watch and wait, for now.

Carefully he pulls the corners of the linen tightly together, then tucks them in. When the corpse is secure, he rises and calls for some servants to help carry it to the tomb he has prepared. The day of death is coming to an end.

Not long ago, this bruised and battered body was a beautiful baby, the Son of God, full of life, wrapped in swaddling clothes, lying in a manger. There, a handful of shepherds and a choir of angels celebrated his birth.

Today, the lifeless corpse is wrapped in white linen, attended by a handful of heavyhearted followers. Angel choirs surely wait in the wings now, songs of celebration on the tips of their tongues. For in the grand scheme of God's eternal plan, weeping may last for the night, but joy will come in the morning.

Respond

There were probably many times Joseph of Arimathea could have spoken out on Christ's behalf. As a member of the Sanhedrin, he attended both trials, watching them slap Jesus around, mocking Him. He never seemed to protest. John tells us that secretly he was a follower of Christ, yet feared the reaction of his peers. Spend some time looking at your own life. Are there times when you fail to speak the truth about Christ? Do you keep quiet when He is maligned, for fear of what others might think? Can you imagine the courage it must have taken for Joseph to reveal his commitment to Christ by asking for the body? In what areas of your walk with God do you long for this kind of courage?

Now consider the women who have never left Jesus' side. See them standing afar, unable to intervene, to even wash the wounds of their beloved teacher. Yet they do not leave. What compels them to stay? What would compel you to commit yourself to Him with such fortitude?

Spend some time in prayer over these things. Read Matthew 10:27–33. Meditate on these things—that which God calls you to speak, that which

God calls you to fear, and the scope of God's concern for your well-being. What is God saying to you? Write a prayer of response.

A Prayer

My Savior, my friend—I can feel the sorrow in Joseph's heart as he wraps your cold body. O what he missed by waiting so long. And how much of you I have not yet understood, or known, or loved because I wait when I could run to you. Banish the foolish fears and selfish passions that keep me from you—burn them like dross until my heart is pure, aflame with desire for you alone, O living God.

38. MYRRH AND ALOES

In the cross is an ocean of love yet unrevealed, a mountain of power still unreleased, and a sea of truth not yet fathomed. . . . There is something utterly exhaustless about the provisions of Calvary.

S. Franklin Logsdon

Reflect

Bring your heart before your heavenly Father today by slowly reading the model prayer found in Matthew 6:9–13. (Say it by heart if you know it.) Reflect on each phrase as you pray it, especially in light of what you have gleaned from contemplating the Cross of Christ.

Read

John 19:39–42; Luke 23:56; and the following narrative.

All Thy garments are fragrant with myrrh and aloes.

Psalm 45:8

With the help of his servants, Joseph of Arimathea carries the corpse of Christ down Golgotha. Travelers stop to stare. Why would a wealthy man such as this become unclean by having anything to do with a dead body, especially that of a criminal?

Two women, Mary of Magdala and Mary the aunt of Jesus, continue to follow, bringing up the rear of the only funeral march he will have. The masses who flocked to hear him teach and watch him perform miracles have disappeared. Those whose bodies were restored by his touch or whose lonely hearts found compassion in his eyes now busy themselves with Sabbath preparations.

Joseph turns at the bottom of the hill and walks several yards to the entrance of a lovely garden against the slope of Golgotha. The scent of spring blossoms fill the air, a pleasant respite to Calvary's rank residue. He directs the men to take the body through an opening carved in the rocky hillside. It is a fairly new sepulcher, no corpse having ever been laid there.

The two women approach, stationing themselves just outside the garden where they can see through the door into the rock-hewn tomb. They watch as Jesus' body is placed on a stone bench protruding from the wall of the cave. But the evening sky grows dim, and they know they must leave. Making plans to return after the Sabbath with spices to anoint their Master, they reluctantly head back toward town.

Joseph removes the linen cloth and begins tenderly to wash the wounded body of Christ in preparation for burial. The process is a source of healing for his own aching heart. As he finishes with the face, a commotion outside

startles him. Peering out, he sees another member of the Sanhedrin entering the garden, followed by several servants bearing jars of rich-scented myrrh and aloes.

He steps outside and as their eyes meet, the two priests sense an unspoken camaraderie. Joseph understands all too well why Nicodemus comes now. He remembers rumors of him meeting with Jesus in the dark of night for religious discussion. He recalls the meeting of the council during the Feast of Tabernacles when Caiaphas demanded Jesus' arrest. Nicodemus spoke boldly then, challenging the high priests to abide by their own laws and not condemn someone without hearing his defense.

Yet like himself, in the mockery of a trial before the Sanhedrin, Nicodemus said nothing in Jesus' favor. When he could have made a difference he kept silent. And like himself, Nicodemus is now compelled to do something—anything. Joseph embraces his friend, kissing him on each cheek.

When the washing is complete, the men quickly expedite the embalming process. They alternate wrapping the body with strips of cloth, then sprinkling the powdered spices over it, leaving the head and face exposed. The aroma of myrrh and aloes allays the stench of decaying flesh. In the remaining minutes of daylight, Joseph wraps and Nicodemus anoints the body of Christ.

When they are finished, they carry the corpse through a low opening into the dark recesses of the cave for final burial. Nicodemus takes a small cloth, saturates it with spices and places it over Jesus' face. It is done.

They step out of the darkness into the cool evening air, where they seize a large boulder and roll it across the entrance to the tomb. Hearts full of grief and regret, the two priests embrace in farewell, hurrying to perform sacred duties and join their families for Sabbath.

The Son of man who had never had a place to lay his head is now put to rest in a rich man's grave. The Lamb whose sacrifice on Calvary drifted like a pleasing aroma to the Father, is now anointed with sweet-smelling

spices fit for a king. As families light the evening candles and pray, the body that held the Light of the world rots in a cold, dark cave. It seems the final act of mankind's greatest tragedy has come to an end.

Respond

Consider the heart of Nicodemus. He was a true seeker who asked sincere questions of Christ when he came to Him at night. How hard it was for him to let go of his religious preconceptions in order to trust the truth of Christ's words. Do you cling to anything today that keeps you from hearing Jesus' voice to you? Religious works? Spiritual busyness? Christian reputation? Ask God to show you what you must leave behind as you come to Jesus in His death.

In the fourth century, the church leader Augustine wrote the following words about his own conversion. Read them slowly, savoring their depth.

> Belatedly I loved thee, O Beauty so ancient and so new, belatedly I loved thee. For see, thou wast within and I was without, and I sought thee out there. Unlovely, I rushed heedlessly among the lovely things thou hast made. Thou wast with me, but I was not with thee.... Thou didst call and cry aloud, and didst force open my deafness. Thou didst gleam and shine, and didst chase away my blindness. Thou didst breathe fragrant odors and I drew in my breath; and now I pant for thee. I tasted, and now I hunger and thirst. Thou didst touch me, and I burned for thy peace.
>
> *Saint Augustine's Confessions*, Book 10

Write a prayer to Jesus, anointing Him with the aromatic spices of your own words.

A Prayer

Lord, they rolled the stone and sealed your body in darkness. It is so hard for me to grasp that it was only a shell—that you were no part of those burial preparations. I see how often I run after things I hope will bring you pleasure, but I am too late, for I've been consumed with dead deeds and lifeless works. I want to learn to hear you in the echoes of silence, dear Lord— to see the flickering flame of love through the darkness of your seeming distance. I don't want to miss you, sweet Savior of mine. I hold my head to your heart and hear the sound of it beating in my ear.

39. THE SABBATH

Nowhere do I more find such fruitful stillness as when I am near the cross. Nowhere do I feel so inclined to take the shoes from off my feet. And how do you account for it?

John Henry Jowett

Reflect

Make this time with God a time of rest as the Jews did on the Sabbath. Mentally cease from all activity except focusing on Him. Breathe deeply and slowly. Feel the coolness of the earth in the dark tomb where Christ has been laid. Smell the aromatic spices. Anticipate the miraculous as you offer yourself to the Savior. Ask Him to reveal His truth to your own heart today.

Read Psalm 24:7–10 aloud as a proclamation of praise and preparation in your own heart for what God will do. Write a prayer to Jesus, opening the way for Him to enter the gates of the various parts of your life.

Read

Luke 23:55–56; Matthew 27:62–66; and the following narrative.

There remains therefore a Sabbath rest for the people of God.

Hebrews 4:9

The setting sun ushers in a high holy day for Jews in Jerusalem as they celebrate both Sabbath and the Feast of Unleavened Bread. Fathers in homes throughout the city regale their children with tales of their ancestors' miraculous Exodus from Egypt long ago.

The forced rest provides much time for reflection and quietness. Even the simplest tasks are left undone, and all of the market stalls owned by Jews have closed until the sun sets tomorrow afternoon. In obedience, both pilgrims who've come to Jerusalem for Passover and those who live here join to keep the Sabbath day holy.

Not everyone rests, however. A small group of women huddle together in one home, consumed with sadness at the events they have witnessed over the past several hours. Every now and then someone asks Mary of Magdala to describe once again what she saw at the tomb owned by the priest named Joseph. Through the long night no one even thinks of trying to sleep.

The men who once followed Christ mourn his death in a room upstairs. It is a sorrowful Sabbath indeed for these whose hope resided in Jesus the teacher. How they grieve. What must they feel? Hopelessness? Disillusionment? Fear? Anger? Does the thought of a future without their beloved Master riddle them with anxiety? Do they second-guess the trust they once had, feeling foolish at their gullibility? Or are they simply numb with shock?

As morning draws near, several members of the Sanhedrin gather in the temple to discuss concerns about the crucified carpenter. Fearing that he will become more of a hero in death than he was in life, Caiaphas determines to demand Pilate's help.

When he hears of the priests arrival, the procurator is put off. He is tired. Over and over last night he awoke, sweating from a nightmare in which his hands were covered with blood and his wife was screaming at him. Hasn't he done everything these zealots want? Why are they bothering him now?

He enters the courtyard, beckoning for Caiaphas to approach. "What is it?"

"Sir, we have been talking and we remember that the deceiver Jesus, when he was still alive, said he would rise again after three days. Of course we don't believe this foolishness, but we are concerned that his disciples might come and steal the body. Then they would tell all our people that he did rise, and things will be worse than when he was alive."

Pilate watches the influential chief priest. He can hardly stand the man with his oily tongue and false humility. But suddenly he is tired of dealing with him. "You may have your guard—go with them and make the grave as secure as you can."

The priests accompany the contingent of Roman soldiers to Joseph's tomb where a stone is already in place. They pull it back, ducking inside to make sure the body is still there. After securing it to their satisfaction, the priests leave the guards in place, returning to the temple for Sabbath sacrifices.

Within the dark bowels of a grave, the empty frame of Jesus rests. But all is not as it seems. While disheartened followers grieve and Pharisees breathe sighs of relief, the Spirit of Christ moves throughout the cosmos, crashing through Hades' gates to proclaim victory over sin and death. In the pit of hell, fallen angels rage at the Son of God who lives after all.

There has never been another Sabbath day like this one. As women are wont to do, Mary and the others channel their pain into plans for embalming the body of Christ. Religious leaders conduct Passover rituals and distraught disciples disappear from sight. But all the while the Lord of the Sabbath

prepares for the event that will soon send shock waves around the world, changing forever the course of history.

Respond

Spend some time imagining the thoughts and feelings of Jesus' followers on this day. Apparently, they had no remembrance or understanding of Jesus' promises concerning His resurrection. All they knew was what they saw in front of them. Can you imagine the despair? The darkness? The lonely ache in their hearts? Try to imagine what it would be like during this time to not have a clue that something wonderful was about to break into your horror.

Thank God for the reality of His presence through His Spirit in your life. Experience His commitment to live within you and work through you. Enjoy the truth that He has chosen you, that He longs for you, and loves to commune with you. Rest for a time with these thoughts.

A Prayer

Mighty Jesus, whirling in Spirit throughout the universe, proclaiming victory, while your followers mourn. I see myself in them, Lord—embracing the dance of death while you declare life. I long to live in the realm where you move and work, though hope seems sealed up in a tomb. Teach me, almighty God, the assurance of things not seen, the confidence of things hoped for—the secret of resurrection faith.

EPILOGUE
THE REST OF THE STORY

*This Man, delivered over by the predetermined plan and
foreknowledge of God, you nailed to a cross by the hands of godless men
and put Him to death. And God raised Him up again, putting an
end to the agony of death, since it was impossible for Him
to be held in its power.*

Acts 2:23–24

Paul Harvey, well-known American radio commentator, is famous for revealing surprise endings to unusual stories and little-known facts about popular news items. He ends every broadcast with the now-famous line: "And that, my friends, is the rest of the story." What might Mr. Harvey say about the nondescript Jew from Nazareth who died on a cross two thousand years ago? Perhaps it would go something like this:

On the third day after his death, Jesus of Nazareth miraculously arose, culminating the fulfillment of over three hundred prophecies from the Hebrew Scriptures. He appeared at least ten times to those who knew Him and to as many as five hundred people at one time. This was no short-lived hallucination on the part of His fanatic followers. He ate with them, exhorted and encouraged them, and let doubters touch the holes in His body from the spear and nails. After forty days He ascended into the clouds in plain view of all, accompanied by angels who promised He would come again one day, in the same manner as He had left.

What of other participants in the drama of Christ's death? The high priest Annas continued a tradition of greed and repression. He raised money by extortion and bribed Roman procurators, all the while proclaiming to represent the holy God. Early records reveal his tomb near the south wall of Jerusalem by the late '60s.

Annas' son-in-law, Caiaphas, enjoyed the longest reign of any chief priest in the first century. He remained a shrewd strategist and politician, enabling his lengthy regime. His family tomb was recently discovered on the south wall of Jerusalem.

Herod Antipas, the Jewish tetrarch, cultivated his friendship with the Roman emperor Tiberius, even building a town in his honor. All the while he sought to expand his own authority, secretly craving the kind of rule his father, Herod Agrippa, had known. In A.D. 39 he was found guilty of treason and banished to Lyones, stripped of all wealth and power. He and his wife, Herodias, died later in Spain.

In Pilate's ten-year reign, he had numerous conflicts with the Jews. One time he overstepped his bounds, having hundreds of Samaritan Jews executed by Roman soldiers. Ordered to return to Rome, he never arrived. Tradition states that while on the way there he committed suicide, not willing to face a Roman trial. The only physical evidence of Pilate's existence are some coins depicting pagan sacrifices produced with his name during his rule in Jerusalem.

The accusers and mockers of Jesus Christ are gone, little more than a footnote in history. In fact, none of them would be worthy of mention were it not for their role in His death.

Yet those who followed Christ made an amazing comeback after He arose. The small band who were too afraid even to attend the Crucifixion were transformed at Pentecost when Jesus poured out His Holy Spirit upon them. Though they faced greater danger and rejection than ever, and in fact all but one were martyred for their faith, they turned the world upside down with their fervor to spread the truth about their Master.

Jesus Christ of Nazareth completely altered the course of history. Even a casual glance at a calendar affirms the reality of his existence two thousand years ago. Everything points to the time before He lived or the time after His death. Today the Christian religion spans the globe, continuing to impact people from every tribe and nation.

No one has ever changed individual lives like Jesus of Nazareth. No one has ever affected the world order like Jesus of Nazareth. He is not only the most unique person of all time, but through the power of His resurrection continues to put hope in the hearts of those looking for life's true meaning.

Perhaps one of the most apt descriptions of Jesus is found every year on Christmas cards all over the world. The author is anonymous, but the words powerful:

> Nineteen wide centuries have come and gone, and today He is the centerpiece of the human race and the leader of the column of progress. I am far within the mark when I say that all the armies that ever marched, and all the navies that were ever built, and all of the parliaments that have ever sat, and all the kings put together that ever reigned have not affected the life of man upon this earth as powerfully as has that one solitary life, Jesus of Nazareth.

And that, my friends, is the rest of the story.

40. RESURRECTION

The disciples had seen the strong hands of God twist the crown of thorns into a crown of glory, and in hands as strong as that they knew themselves safe. . . . They had expected a walkover, and they beheld a victory; they had expected an earthly Messiah, and they beheld the Soul of Eternity.

Dorothy L. Sayers

Reflect

Today is a day of victory and celebration—a confirmation of the hope that we have in our hearts through the Holy Spirit who lives there. Begin with a time of thanksgiving for all God has done for you, especially in view of the Cross.

Read or sing the words to the following hymn, offering a heart of deep joy and awe-filled worship.

Crown Him With Many Crowns
Matthew Bridges and Godfrey Thring

Crown Him with many crowns,
The Lamb upon His throne:
Hark! how the heavenly anthem drowns
All music but its own!
Awake, my soul, and sing
Of Him who died for thee,
And hail Him as thy matchless King
Thru all eternity.

Crown Him the Lord of love:
Behold His hands and side—
Rich wounds, yet visible above,
In beauty glorified;
No angel in the sky
Can fully bear that sight,
But downward bends his wond'ring eye
At mysteries so bright.

Crown Him the Lord of life;
Who triumphed o'er the grave,
Who rose victorious to the strife
For those He came to save;
His glories now we sing,
Who died and rose on high,
Who died eternal life to bring
And lives that death may die.

Crown Him the Lord of heav'n:
One with the Father known,
One with the Spirit thru Him giv'n
From yonder glorious throne.
To Thee be endless praise,
For Thou for us hast died;
Be Thou, O Lord, thru endless days
Adored and magnified.

Read

Mark 16:1; Matthew 28:2–4; Luke 24:1–11; John 20:2–18; and the following narrative.[1]

I have seen the Lord.

John 20:18

When the last of Saturday's sun sinks below the horizon, the long Sabbath ends, propelling the women into action. Three go to purchase more supplies while the marketplace is still open. Upon their return, tender hands

crush and mix dried flowers and pungent spices for hours, all of them soberly sharing this final act of compassion.

When morning nears, they hurry off to the tomb. After walking some distance, one of the women suggests they will have trouble rolling away the stone from the grave, and a discussion ensues concerning whether they should get one of the men. But they are almost there, and no one wants to turn back now.

In the predawn darkness, soldiers stand and stretch, tired from the long night. As the morning watch moves into position, the ground begins to shake under their feet. In astonishment the guards see a dazzling creature descending from heaven. With a face like lightning and clothed in brilliant white, the angel rolls the stone away, taking a seat at the top.

In an instant the guards faint as though dead. Within a few seconds they awake, rushing frantically into the tomb. Panic grips them as they see no trace of a body. The entire group races back toward Jerusalem, terrified at what they have seen, dreading Pilate's response.

The sun creeps across the eastern sky, though the tomb is still shrouded in darkness as the women arrive. Astounded that the stone is removed from the sepulcher's entrance, two of them go inside, shocked at what they see. The body of Jesus is not there.

Suddenly the cave is bathed in light and two men in shining robes dazzle the women. Falling in fear to the ground, the words they hear stun them.

"Why are you looking in a tomb for someone who is alive? He is not here—he is risen! Don't you remember what he said—that the Messiah must be betrayed by evil men and be crucified, and that he would rise again on the third day?"

The women glance at each other, then burst from the cave. Followed by the others, they run back to Jerusalem where the disciples continue to mourn. Breathless, they tell the men what they have just seen.

The disciples look at them as if they are crazy, dismissing their words as

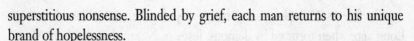

superstitious nonsense. Blinded by grief, each man returns to his unique brand of hopelessness.

Mary Magdalene cannot believe their response. She pleads with Peter and John to believe her. "They have taken the Lord's body—it is gone, and I don't know where they have placed it."

Something in her voice stirs them. They hurry from the house, through the streets of the city to the tomb of Joseph of Arimathea. John, being younger and faster, arrives first. He bends down and sees the empty cloths, but stays back, afraid. Peter catches up quickly and crashes into the cave, determined to find the truth.

There on the stone bench lie the linen cloths, completely undisturbed, as if the body simply disappeared within the folds. On the side lies the head-piece in a tidy roll. Slowly, faith begins to fill the crevices of Peter's broken heart.

John cautiously enters the cave and together they share a moment of pure incredulity. Words from the past echo through their minds. The Rabbi had told them he would rise again—could it be? Is it possible? Can they dare hope? Thoughtfully they walk in silence back to town.

Mary Magdalene, having followed them to the tomb, watches them leave. She begins to weep, stooping down one more time to see the empty grave. But it isn't empty. On either end of the bench, where she'd seen them lay the body of Christ, are two white-robed angels.

"Why do you cry?" one asks.

"Because they've taken my Lord away, and I don't know where they put him."

Sobbing by now, Mary hears a sound behind her. She looks over her shoulder, and the sight of a gardener gives her a glimmer of hope. "Sir, please—if you have taken him away, just tell me where, and I will go and get him."

"Mary."

She freezes. Only one person has ever spoken her name like that before. Long ago, when tortured by demons, Jesus of Nazareth called her "Mary" and set her free. The scene flashes through her mind as she turns to face the one who speaks.

"Master!" Mary exclaims, rushing toward him.

"Wait, Mary, you cannot cling to me now for I haven't yet ascended to my Father. You must go and find my brothers. Tell them that I ascend to my Father and your Father, my God and your God."

Then he is gone. Mary stands for a moment in complete amazement at what she has seen and heard. Tears stream down her cheeks as she goes to the disciples. One by one and in small groups she comes upon those who once walked with Christ.

"*I have seen the Lord,*" she tells them. The look in her eyes and wonder in her voice leaves no room for doubt that, indeed, she has encountered the risen Christ.

I have seen the Lord. Resurrection hope is spawned in that moment, then spreads like a soothing ointment to those who will believe—some having seen, and others simply by faith—that what Jesus of Nazareth said he would do, he did. And resurrection hope transcends time, instilling eternity in the hearts of mankind.

Respond

Can you even comprehend what Mary must have felt when she heard the voice of Jesus saying her name as only He could say it? Stop and sense the wonder, the joy, the hope that must have encompassed her complete being. Place yourself there in that time, bringing with you all your fears, your unfulfilled dreams, your disappointments, and griefs. Hear Jesus speaking your name. Listen. Hear it again.

Fall at His feet and worship Him. Say aloud, "I have seen the Lord." Now see yourself running to those you know and those you don't know.

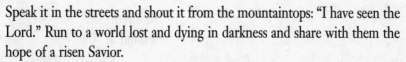

Speak it in the streets and shout it from the mountaintops: "I have seen the Lord." Run to a world lost and dying in darkness and share with them the hope of a risen Savior.

Celebrate! Rejoice! Sing! Shout! Jump for joy! Dance with all your might! The Lord lives! He is worthy! Give thanks! Give Him the honor and praise due His Holy name! HE IS RISEN! ALLELUIA! For the Lord God Omnipotent Reigns!

A Prayer

O my Master, simple joy so fills my heart that I have no words to speak. You are not dead. You are alive! You have defeated death. And I, too, will live with you for eternity. How I long for the day when I will see you face-to-face, dearest Redeemer. I will kiss your nail-scarred feet again and again and I will touch your wounded side, holding your precious hands to my face. There I will stay, proclaiming forever, "I have seen the Lord."

Notes

1. Once again, each Gospel author includes the parts of the story important to their divinely inspired emphasis. It is difficult to put them together chronologically, as attested to by hundreds of scholarly works on this issue. I have sought to incorporate as much detail as possible without losing the simplicity of the Resurrection story.

RESOURCES

Adels, Jill Haak. *The Wisdom of the Saints*. New York: Oxford University Press, 1987.

Bishop, Jim. *The Day Christ Died*. San Francisco: HarperSanFrancisco, 1957.

Barbet, Pierre, M.D. *A Physician at Calvary*. Translated by the Earl of Wicklow. New York: P. J. Kennedy & Sons, 1953.

Brown, Raymond E. *The Death of the Messiah: From Gethsemane to the Grave*, Vols. 1 & 2. New York: Doubleday, 1994.

Card, Michael. *Immanuel: Reflections on the Life of Christ*. Nashville: Thomas Nelson, 1990.

Cantalamessa, Raniero. *Life in the Lordship of Christ*. St. Louis: Sheed & Ward, 1990.

Chambers, J. Oswald. *My Utmost for His Highest*. New York: Dodd, Mead & Company, 1935.

———. *The Place of Help*. Fort Washington, Pa.: Christian Literature Crusade, 1935.

———. *The Philosophy of Sin*. Fort Washington, Pa.: Christian Literature Crusade, 1960.

Davis, C. Truman, M.D. "A Physician Testifies About the Crucifixion," *The Review of the NEWS*, April 14, 1976.

Edersheim, Alfred. *Jesus the Messiah*. New York: Longmans, Green & Company, 1898.

Edwards, William D., M.D.; Wesley J. Gabel, M.Div.; Floyd Hosmer. "On the Physical Death of Jesus Christ," *The Journal of the American Medical Association*, March 21, 1986, Vol. 256.

Fosbroke, Hughell. *By Means of Death*. Conn.: Seabury Press, 1956.

Hession, Roy. *We Would See Jesus*. Fort Washington, Pa.: Christian Literature Crusade, 1958.

Kiehl, Erich H. *The Passion of Our Lord*. Grand Rapids: Baker Book House, 1990.

Logsdon, S. Franklin. *Lingering at Calvary*. Chicago: Moody Bible Institute, 1956.

Manning, Brennan. *The Signature of Jesus on the Pages of Our Lives*. Eugene, Ore.: Multnomah, 1992.

March, R. E. *The Greatest Theme in the World*. New York: Gospel Publishing House, 1908.

McGrath, Alister E. *The Mystery of the Cross*. Grand Rapids: Zondervan, 1988.

Morris, Leon. *The Cross of Jesus*. Grand Rapids: Eerdmans Publishing Co., 1988.

———. *The Atonement: It's Meaning and Significance*. England: InterVarsity Press, 1983.

———. *The Apostolic Preaching of the Cross*. London: The Tyndale Press, 1955.

Motter, Alton M. *Preaching the Passion*. Philadelphia: Fortress Press, 1963.

Murray, Andrew. *The Blood of the Cross*. New Jersey: Fleming Revell, n.d.

———. *The Cross of Christ*. Grand Rapids: Zondervan, 1989.

Murphy, Richard T. A. *Days of Glory: The Passion, Death, and Resurrection of Jesus Christ*. Grand Rapids: Servant Books, 1980.

Rhodes, Tricia McCary. *Soul at Rest*. Minneapolis: Bethany House Publishers, 1996.

Robertson, A. T. *A Harmony of the Gospels*. New York: Harper & Row, 1950.

Slaughter, Frank G. *The Crown and the Cross*. New York: World Publishing Company, 1960.

Stott, John R. *The Cross of Christ*. Chicago: InterVarsity Press, 1986.

Wiersbe, Warren, ed. *Classic Sermons on the Cross of Christ*. Grand Rapids: Kregel Publications, 1990.

Wangerin, Walter Jr. *The Book of God: The Bible as a Novel*. Grand Rapids: Zondervan, 1996.

———. *Reliving the Passion*. Grand Rapids: Zondervan, 1992.

Whyte, Alexander. *The Best of Alexander Whyte*. Grand Rapids: 1953.

BOOKS BY
TRICIA McCARY RHODES

The Soul at Rest: A Journey Into Contemplative Prayer
Contemplating the Cross

Contemplating the

CROSS